ERRATUM

The photos published on the following pages of the present book have been given a wrong attribution by the author due to a practical mistake: 11, 47, 55, 67, 70, 123, 126, 127, 129, 130, 135 (lower), 138 (upper) and 158 (both). The correct attribution for these photos is: (*Photo and copyright by The Vikings of Bjornstad*).

Armies of the Vikings,
AD 793–1066

Armies of the Vikings, AD 793–1066

History, Organization and Equipment

Gabriele Esposito

Pen & Sword
MILITARY

First published in Great Britain in 2021
by Pen & Sword Military
An imprint of Pen & Sword Books Limited
47 Church Street
Barnsley
South Yorkshire
S70 2AS

ISBN 978 1 39900 839 6

A CIP catalogue record for this book is
available from the British Library

Typeset in Adobe Caslon
by Mac Style

Printed and bound in India by Replika Press Pvt. Ltd.

Pen & Sword Books Limited incorporates the imprints of Atlas,
Archaeology, Aviation, Discovery, Family History, Fiction, History, Maritime,
Military, Military Classics, Politics, Select, Transport, True Crime, Air World,
Frontline Publishing, Leo Cooper, Remember When, Seaforth Publishing,
The Praetorian Press, Wharncliffe Local History, Wharncliffe Transport,
Wharncliffe True Crime and White Owl.

For a complete list of Pen & Sword titles please contact
PEN & SWORD BOOKS LIMITED
47 Church Street, Barnsley, South Yorkshire, S70 2AS, England
E-mail: enquiries@pen-and-sword.co.uk
Website: www. pen-and-sword.co.uk

Contents

Gabriele Esposito is a military historian who works as a freelance author and researcher for some of the most important publishing houses in the military history sector. In particular, he is an expert specializing in uniformology: his interests and expertise range from the ancient civilizations to modern post-colonial conflicts. During recent years he has conducted and published several researches on the military history of the Latin American countries, with special attention on the War of the Triple Alliance and the War of the Pacific. He is among the leading experts on the military history of the Italian Wars of Unification and the Spanish Carlist Wars. His books and essays are published on a regular basis by Osprey Publishing, Winged Hussar Publishing and Libreria Editrice Goriziana; he is also the author of numerous military history articles appearing in specialized magazines like *Ancient Warfare Magazine*, *Medieval Warfare Magazine*, *Classic Arms & Militaria Magazine*, *History of War*, *Guerres et Histoire*, *Focus Storia* and *Focus Storia Wars*.

Acknowledgements

This book is dedicated to my magnificent parents, Maria Rosaria and Benedetto, for the immense love and fundamental support that they always give me. It is thanks to their precious advice over many years that the present book has been much improved. Very special thanks goes to Philip Sidnell, the commissioning editor of my books for Pen & Sword: his love for history and his passion for publishing are the key factors behind the success of our publications. Many thanks also to the production manager of this title, Matt Jones, for his excellent work and great enthusiasm. A special acknowledgement goes to Tony Walton, for the editing of this book with his usual passion and competence, as well as for honouring me with his sincere friendship. A very special mention goes to the brilliant re-enactment groups that collaborated with their photos to the creation of this book: without the incredible work of research of their members, the final result of this publication would have not been the same. As a result, I want to express my deep gratitude to the following living history associations: Joinsborg Vikings Hird from Poland, Brokkar Lag from Spain, Sjórvaldar Vikings from the United States of America and Confraternita del Leone/Historia Viva from Italy.

Introduction

The Vikings are without doubt one of the most 'iconic' peoples of the Middle Ages. Their ferocious raids and rapid incursions were a major part of European history for almost three centuries, and they are still remembered today as one of the most characteristic elements of the time. It should be noted, however, that the Vikings were much more than simple raiders who terrorized most of medieval Europe: they were a people of navigators and explorers with incredible skills, who crossed the oceans and navigated the rivers of the northern hemisphere in search of new lands to settle and live in prosperity. Viking expansionism and migrations involved large portions of the known world in the central centuries of the Middle Ages. Moving from their homeland in southern Scandinavia, the Vikings first settled in the British Isles before advancing further west. They reached Iceland and Greenland after crossing the Atlantic Ocean, populating islands that had never before been visited by any European. From their new outposts, the Scandinavian explorers were able to move even further west, reaching the coastline of present-day Canada and establishing a short-lived settlement in North America that was known as Vinland. The Vikings were consequently the first Europeans to live in the Americas and the first navigators to understand the great extent of the Atlantic Ocean (which had always been considered as the 'edge of the world' by most ancient civilizations).

The Viking presence in Britain and Ireland was characterized by continuous conflicts with the local populations, who saw the Scandinavian newcomers as deadly rivals. In Britain, after decades of incessant fights against the Saxons, the Vikings created their own short-lived domain known as the Danelaw. In Ireland, however, they were utterly defeated by the local Celtic communities after having obtained control over large portions of the island. To the east of Scotland, the Vikings were able to establish a long-lasting realm that was known as the Kingdom of the Isles, which comprised the Hebrides, the Isle of Man and the islands of the Firth of Clyde. This realm continued to exist until the mid-thirteenth century and was a long-lasting presence on the political scene of the British Isles. It should be noted that, during the period taken into account in this book, the Vikings also exerted their control over the Orkney Islands and the Shetland Islands, to the point that their influence over these peripheral areas of Britain was a very significant one.

In Western Europe, the Scandinavian explorers and conquerors had several targets, most notably the territories of the former Frankish Empire. The latter had lost its territorial unity soon after the death of its founder, Charlemagne, and thus was an easy prey for the Vikings, who raided northern France very frequently and ravaged key regions of the country such as Normandy and Brittany. The newly born Kingdom of France was never able to counter them effectively, which resulted in the famous Viking siege of Paris. Eventually, in order to save the central region of their kingdom, the French monarchs had no choice but to cede Normandy to the Scandinavian pirates. In their new French homeland, the Vikings soon flourished, gradually transforming themselves into feudal aristocrats. However, they never lost their original spirit of conquest, and during the following decades moved from Normandy to conquer England and southern Italy. The warriors who triumphed at Hastings in 1066 and who conquered southern Italy during the early eleventh century, however, were very different from their Viking ancestors: they were not more sea-raiders armed with axes, they were feudal heavy knights with highly skilled training and discipline. Within a few decades, the Vikings of Normandy had transformed themselves and started to be known as Normans.

In Eastern Europe, where they were called Varangians, the Vikings obtained incredible results in a very short time. Moving from Sweden, they settled in the Baltic (for example in Estonia and Finland) before exploring the courses of the great Russian rivers. In just a few decades they colonized an immense portion of present-day Russia and Ukraine, subjugating the local tribes of Slavs and establishing the first centralized realm in the history of that region of Europe: the immense Grand Principality of Kievan Rus or Kievan Rus', stretching from Novgorod on the Baltic Sea to the Black Sea in southern Ukraine. Russia, or the 'Land of the Rus', was dominated for a long period by a Varangian elite, who were strong enough to menace the Byzantine Empire to the south. Like their French equivalents, the Byzantine monarchs had no choice to save their realm but to find a compromise with the Scandinavians: they sent large amounts of gold to the Grand Principality of Kievan Rus and created a strong military corps of mercenary Scandinavians that became known as the Varangian Guard. The latter became part of the Byzantine Imperial Guard and soon earned a reputation as a legendary combat corps.

This book will describe all the most important military campaigns fought by the Vikings and will analyze their military organization, as well as their traditional panoply of weapons. The analysis will start from the first documented Viking raid of 793 and will end with the crucial year 1066, which was a very significant one for the history of the Scandinavian warriors. Two simultaneous invasions of England took place in 1066: a Viking one in the north that was defeated, and a Norman one in the south that was victorious. The events of that crucial year definitively showed that the Vikings were the past and that their Norman heirs were the future. Gradually, during the eleventh century, the Vikings of Scandinavia lost most of their distinctive characters as they adopted the Christian faith and a feudal organization almost simultaneously. Denmark, Norway and Sweden were all organized as proper kingdoms, and the traditions of the Vikings were gradually marginalized. The situation was somewhat different in Eastern Europe, where the Kievan Rus' continued to flourish until being broken up into smaller states due to internal divisions. The Varangian Guard also continued, but, ironically, from 1066 it started to comprise an increasing number of Saxon warriors who had abandoned their homeland as refugees after the Battle of Hastings.

Despite all the changes described above, the Scandinavian nations of Denmark, Norway and Sweden have always retained some distinctive Viking nature that can still be seen to this day. The same can be said for Iceland and Greenland, two islands that were populated by the Vikings and whose culture is largely a Scandinavian one.

Chapter 1

The Origins of the Vikings

The terms 'Vikings' and 'Varangians' are commonly used to identify those Scandinavian raiders who operated across Europe during the period 800–1000; the first term is very popular in Western Europe, while the second is employed in Eastern Europe. It should be noted that all the Vikings belonged to the larger group of the Norsemen, a North Germanic ethno-linguistic group that spoke the Old Norse language and lived in the southern part of Scandinavia. Their homeland comprised present-day Denmark as well as the southern parts of Norway and Sweden. From a cultural point of view, the Norsemen had a lot in common with the South Germanic tribes who invaded the Roman Empire during the last centuries of Antiquity. Differently from the southern Germani, however, they had always had very little contact with the most advanced civilizations of Continental or Mediterranean Europe such as the Celts or the Romans. As a result, the material culture of the Norsemen was quite 'primitive' if judged through the eyes of a more civilized European from the Mediterranean area. In many respects, the Norsemen had remained at an earlier phase in the evolutive process that had transformed the Germani of the south into an advanced civilization.

Like the earlier South Germanic tribes, the Norsemen were skilled warriors and lived in small rural villages. They knew how to work metals in order to produce formidable weapons, but did not practice agriculture on a very large scale. Their lands were difficult to reach for foreign merchants, and the natural environment in which they lived was particularly harsh; their economy was thus very simple and they had no monetary system. During the long centuries of the Roman Empire, their only direct contact with the regions of Southern Europe was through the commerce of amber, a precious material that could be found only around the Baltic Sea. The Norsemen knew very little of the rest of the world, and were too few to represent a driving force in the new world that was emerging from the end of Antiquity.

Over time, however, the situation described above started to change very rapidly, and an increasing number of Norsemen began to leave their homeland in order to travel abroad in search of new lands to raid or to colonize. Those Norsemen who changed their usual lifestyle to become pirates and explorers started to be known as Vikings or Varangians. Consequently, we can say that all Vikings were Norsemen,

Western Viking with chainmail and spear. (*Photo and copyright by Sjórvaldar Vikings*)

Eastern Viking with fur cap and spear. (*Photo and copyright by Jomsborg Vikings Hird*)

but that only some Norsemen were Vikings. The expansion of the Norsemen across Northern Europe began during the very last decades of the eighth century, in an age that saw the ascendancy of the Frankish Empire in Continental Europe and the end of Arab expansionism across the Mediterranean. The causes that determined the emergence of the Vikings are many, and are still a matter of discussion among modern scholars, with each of them having some importance in creating a radical change in the traditional society of the Norsemen.

Before the beginning of the so-called 'Viking Age', southern Scandinavia endured a great demographic expansion that was mostly caused by climatic changes. Indeed, until the middle of the eighth century, the climate of countries like Denmark or Norway was too cold to permit the existence of a large population since it significantly limited agricultural production. By 750, this situation had started to change, the climate becoming less cold and the population thus starting to expand thanks to an enlarged production of food supplies. In just a few decades, the demographic situation of Scandinavia changed dramatically, to the point that the region began experiencing all the problems related to over-population. The agricultural capacity of the land was not enough to keep up with the increasing population, and thus many Norsemen found themselves without means of sustainment. The number of individuals who had no land and no personal properties grew, especially once all the cultivable lands had been occupied. The sudden demographic boom produced a mass of landless men who were in search of material wealth in order to feed their families, or of new territories where to settle as farmers. These individuals had no choice but to leave their homeland in search of new opportunities, operating as pirates or crossing the seas as explorers. Unlike the southern Germanic communities, the Norsemen were skilled navigators and knew how to build the most effective ships of the Middle Ages. Consequently, travelling long distances across the oceans or following the course of rivers for thousands of miles was not a problem for them.

A demographic boom was undoubtedly the primary reason for Viking expansionism, but several other changes also took place in Scandinavia during the eighth century. First of all, iron became more common in the area due to the opening of new mines where this vital material could be extracted. The new and increasing amounts of iron were used to produce more effective weapons, as well as new agricultural tools that augmented the productivity of the Norse farmers. In addition, during those same years, the Norsemen improved their sea-faring capabilities by perfecting the design of their ships, with larger sails introduced together with new tacking practices. Thanks to these innovations and the fact that they learned how to sail at night by following the stars, the Norsemen could start planning ambitious raids and expeditions.

Western Viking equipped with spear and shield. (*Photo and copyright by Jomsborg Vikings Hird*)

Western Viking with hood
and axe. (*Photo and copyright
by Jomsborg Vikings Hird*)

When the Viking Age began, no central government existed in the Scandinavian countries of Denmark, Sweden and Norway: each tribal group had its supreme leader, and thus there was no political entity that could control Viking expansionism in a centralized way. All the Norsemen were still pagans, the Christian faith not yet being practised north of Charlemagne's domains. When the Vikings started launching their first raids, their primary target in the west was the British Isles, since most of Continental Europe was under the firm military control of the Carolingians. The latter had a very strong military apparatus and a centralized administration that could effectively defend its territory. The military and political situation of Britain and Ireland, on the other hand, was completely different, being characterized by widespread fragmentation. England was populated by the Anglo-Saxons, who had crossed the English Channel some centuries before and had created their own small realms after crushing the resistance of the Romano-British communities. For several decades, until Alfred the Great unified the country in 886, England was divided into seven small kingdoms that were constantly at war against each other, and which were collectively known as the 'Heptarchy': East Anglia, Mercia, Northumbria, Wessex, Essex, Kent and Sussex. The Vikings were well aware that these kingdoms were very weak from a military point of view if attacked singly, and thus nurtured the ambition of one day conquering the whole territory of England. The island of England was a very rich land, full of natural resources and perfect for agriculture: by conquering it, the Scandinavians would have resolved all their problems related to over-population. To the west of Anglo-Saxon England there were the small Celtic realms of Wales, which had been able to stop the expansionism of the Saxons during the previous decades but which were too fragmented from a political point of view to represent a significant military entity. Around 780, there were five main princedoms in Wales: Gwynedd, Powys, Dyfed, Gwent and Dumnonia. These were all inhabited by the direct heirs of the Romano-British communities who fought against the Saxons in England and had a distinctive culture. To the north of the Heptarchy there was Scotland, which had long been inhabited by a confederation of Celtic peoples who were known as Picts. The latter had fought lengthy wars with the Romans and had launched devastating raids across England. The leading group among the Picts was that of the Fortriu, which dominated over the other minor communities. There were, however, two smaller and independent kingdoms on the territory of present-day western Scotland that were not controlled by the Picts: the Kingdom of Dál Riata and the Kingdom of Strathclyde. The former was inhabited by Scoti coming from Ireland, while the latter was populated by Britons, who had a lot in common with the Celtic communities of Wales. Compared with the Anglo-Saxons of England, however, the Picts were less fragmented from a political point of view since they controlled most of Scotland. Ireland was inhabited by the Scoti or Gaels, another confederation of Celtic peoples who had a lot in common with the Picts. The original alliance existing between the Scoti and the Picts was gradually destroyed by internal rivalries, and the establishment of the Kingdom of Dál Riata in western Scotland led to several conflicts between the two communities. The Scoti of Ireland were extremely fragmented politically, since their clans were organized as independent princedoms and were constantly at war against each other. There were six small realms in Ireland by the beginning of the Viking raids: Munster, Leinster, Connacht, Airgialla, Uí Néill and Ulaid. Like the Anglo-Saxon states of the Heptarchy, these were frequently ravaged by civil wars, and every now and then one of them emerged as a 'regional' power.

Chapter 2

The Early Raids in England and the Great Heathen Army

The first Vikings appeared in England in 789, when three of their ships sailed to the Isle of Portland in Dorset. These few Scandinavians were mistaken for merchants by a local royal official, and thus were asked to pay a trading tax on the goods that they were transporting; offended by the request, the Scandinavians murdered the royal official and left the island without committing other crimes. It seems that this early episode of Viking violence in England was just the result of an 'explorative mission' that was carried out in view of future expeditions. The real starting point of the Viking raids against England, however, is marked by the famous attack that was launched against the Holy Island of Lindisfarne in 793. Lindisfarne, located off the coast of Northumbria, was one of the most important religious sites of Anglo-Saxon England: its monastery was extremely rich and its monastic community exerted a strong influence over north-eastern England. The Vikings knew full well that the island and monastery were full of treasures, and that Lindisfarne could be attacked very easily from the sea. The Scandinavians landed on the island without encountering opposition and took the local community by surprise. Being pagans, they showed no respect for the monks and killed all the people they encountered. The whole of Christian Europe was shocked by the events at Lindisfarne: a group of violent 'pagan devils' had razed to the ground a holy monastery after killing many monks and civilians to steal the treasures that were preserved in a peaceful religious site. The events of 793 had an enormous psychological impact over the inhabitants of Northumbria: a new deadly menace was appearing on the horizon for England, and the Anglo-Saxon kingdoms were not ready to face it.

In 794, a small Viking fleet attacked the rich monastery of Jarrow in Northumbria. This time the raiders encountered strong resistance and some of their leaders were killed during fighting; unexpectedly, they were forced to leave without capturing treasures or slaves. Following their defeat, the Scandinavian raiders had their ships beached at Tynemouth and were all massacred by the locals, who had been alerted by the attack on Jarrow. Unlike what had happened in 793, this second Viking expedition against an English monastery had been a total failure. The Scandinavians had attacked with a very limited number of men and had been beaten off by the strong resistance of the locals. They had also suffered from a lack of knowledge of the

Western Viking archer. (*Photo and copyright by Jomsborg Vikings Hird*)

Western Viking armed with heavy spear and axe. (*Photo and copyright by Sjórvaldar Vikings*)

coastline along which they were operating, and had consequently been slaughtered after the failure of their assault. It was clear from these first two Viking attacks in England that the Scandinavian raiders of this early phase preferred to assault isolated religious sites where they could plunder and capture slaves without encountering any serious resistance. It was for these reasons that they conducted their expeditions with a very limited number of ships. Following the raid against Jarrow, the Vikings continued to attack English targets, but only infrequently. Monasteries and minster churches remained their favourite targets as they contained valuable objects that could be easily transported on their ships. They also started at this time to direct their incursions against Scotland and Ireland. They realized that to pillage England they needed to organize their incursions in a more effective way from a military and logistical point of view. In 840, the Scandinavians organized a new expedition against England, which had as its primary target the Kingdom of Wessex. This time the raiders assembled a large army that was made up of several different war bands and which was transported on thirty-five ships. The Vikings had learned from past experience that small expeditions involving just a few ships could achieve only very limited results and invest isolated sites only for a short time. Aethelwulf, the king of Wessex, moved against the Vikings at the head of his army but was defeated after three days of bloody fighting at the Battle of Carhampton in Somerset. This was the first major pitched clash fought in England between Scandinavians and Saxons and was the first important victory obtained by the Vikings outside their homeland.

After defeating Aethelwulf, the Vikings were free to plunder Somerset for several days without meeting any serious opposition, killing hundreds of people and capturing many slaves. It should be remembered that the Vikings also conducted their incursions to capture young people who could be put to work in the Scandinavian fields, which served to increase the terror of the local Saxon communities living in the areas exposed to Viking raids. During the years 840–860, the Scandinavian raiders continued to attack the Kingdom of Wessex, whose military resources had been severely curtailed by their defeat at Carhampton. Aethelwulf, however, gradually learned how to deal with the Viking raids, and was able to repulse several of them after gaining some minor victories. Sporadic Scandinavian attacks against England continued at this time, but the Battle of Carhampton had shown the Vikings that the Saxon realms were too weak to repulse a properly organized seaborne invasion. As a result, the Scandinavian pirates decided to change their strategy, abandoning the practice of conducting small local incursions in favour of organizing larger invasions. Around 860, all the various Viking war leaders who had conducted raids in England decided to assemble their forces and create a large fleet to invade Saxon lands. The new Viking military force soon became known in England as the 'Great Heathen Army'. It comprised several thousand warriors and was mostly made up of Danes, along with contingents from Norway and Sweden. Instead of landing in Wessex, as they had done several times during the previous decades, the leaders of the Great Heathen Army decided to attack East Anglia and Kent.

The long-planned Scandinavian invasion of England took place in 865, after several minor attacks conducted against the Kingdom of Northumbria. The Great Heathen Army landed on the Isle of Thanet in Kent, which was quickly transformed into an important operational base for the Vikings. The people of Kent tried to come to terms with the invaders, offering them the payment of a special tribute (which became known as 'danegeld') in exchange for peace. But the Vikings would not accept any form of payment and started to pillage the eastern portion of Kent with brutal violence. Following these events, the Kingdom of East Anglia made peace with the Vikings, who had by now established a permanent base in Kent. In exchange for horses and food supplies, the Vikings did not ravage the territory of East Anglia, where they spent the winter of 865/866 before moving north to invest the Kingdom of Northumbria. The military forces of Northumbria were easily defeated by the Scandinavians, who obtained danegeld from the local population and even placed their own 'puppet' monarch on the throne of Northumbria.

After building up a major new base at York, the Vikings moved against the Kingdom of Mercia, where they captured Nottingham in 867. Burgred, the monarch of Mercia, quickly understood that he had no choice but to form an alliance with the Kingdom of Wessex in order to repulse the Great Heathen Army, which was too strong to be defeated by a single Saxon army. The combined military forces of Mercia and Wessex besieged Nottingham for some time, but failed to achieve any significant result. Consequently, Burgred decided to surrender and accepted the payment of the danegeld to the Vikings. The Great Heathen Army remained in York in 868–869 after having defeated or submitted Kent, East Anglia, Northumbria and Mercia. During the early months of 870, however, hostilities resumed between the Scandinavians and East Anglia. The king of the East Anglians, Edmund, had understood the long-term risks related to the creation of a stable Viking kingdom in England, and thus strove to stop the expansion of the invaders. A series of bloody battles were fought between Edmund and the Vikings, which were all won by the Scandinavians. Edmund was captured and tortured before being killed, leaving East Anglia open for Scandinavian settlement. In the summer of 871, a new Viking army, known as the 'Great Summer Army' and consisting of several thousand warriors, landed in England to secure the Scandinavian possessions. With the arrival of these reinforcements, the Vikings decided to continue their expansion by turning their attention to the Kingdom of Wessex. The latter was now ruled by Aethelred, who could count on the support of his younger brother, Alfred.

Western Viking archer. (*Photo and copyright by Jomsborg Vikings Hird*)

Western Viking equipped with axe and shield. Note the Gjermundbu Helmet. (*Photo and copyright by Confraternita del Leone/Historia Viva*)

Chapter 3

The Ascendancy and Fall of the Danelaw

On 8 January 871, the Battle of Ashdown took place in Berkshire between the Vikings and the Saxons of Wessex. The major clash took place at a location that was chosen by the Scandinavian warriors, who could deploy themselves on high ground. During the battle, Alfred – the future Alfred the Great – showed all his courage and great military capabilities, launching a violent frontal attack against the dominant positions of the enemy and crushing the Viking line after some very harsh fighting. The Scandinavians suffered heavy losses during the battle and were closely pursued by Alfred during the following night. The important success obtained by the Saxons at Ashdown stopped the Vikings for some time and saved Wessex from destruction, but it was not a decisive victory. After only a few weeks, the Scandinavians resumed their offensive and obtained two minor victories at Basing and Meretun. Three months after the Battle of Ashdown, Alfred became King of Wessex after the sudden death of his brother. The new monarch, after having been defeated at Basing and Meretun, was in no condition to continue the fight against the invaders, who by now enjoyed a great numerical superiority in warriors. In order to reorganize his military forces and formulate new alliances with the other English kings, Alfred needed time, so he paid large sums of money to the Vikings in order to suspend hostilities and save his realm from the devastations of war.

After ending their campaign in Wessex, the Scandinavians became heavily involved in Northumbria, where they had to crush a rebellion by the local population. The uprising was easily suppressed, after which the Vikings restored their puppet ruler on the throne of Northumbria. Over time, the Scandinavian presence in England became more stable, with the Vikings exerting direct or indirect control over four of the major Anglo-Saxon kingdoms. However, a new sense of 'national' unity was developing among the English communities thanks to the brilliant leadership of Alfred. The Saxons were becoming aware that only by uniting all their military resources could they expel the Vikings from their lands.

In 874, the Scandinavians strengthened their occupation of Mercia and expelled the local king. The Vikings then divided their strong military forces into two parts: one marched north from Northumbria to Scotland in order to pillage as much as they could, while the other established a new operational base at Cambridge in view of further expansionist moves. Initially, Alfred of Wessex tried to maintain peaceful

relations with the Scandinavians, but his attempts were unsuccessful as the Vikings had decided to invest his realm. The Great Heathen Army raided large areas of Wessex from 875–878, causing serious losses to the local population and devastating much of the countryside. In order to save his military forces and to gain time for further preparations, Alfred fell back to the inhospitable Marsh of Athelney in Somerset, where he was protected from enemy attacks by the harsh nature of the local terrain.

After having reorganized his troops, Alfred finally gave battle at Edington in Wiltshire. The decisive clash took place in May 878, with the forces of the monarch of Wessex facing those of the Viking leader Guthrum the Old. Very few details are known about the Battle of Edington, but it seems that it started with a massive Scandinavian attack that was repulsed by the Saxons, who deployed themselves in a strong defensive formation. After the Viking assault was crushed, a violent Saxon counter-attack decided the outcome of the clash in favour of Alfred. The Vikings suffered heavy losses and the few survivors of their army were surrounded by the Saxons. The Scandinavians, who had suffered their first serious defeat in England after decades of victorious raids, sued for peace and sent several hostages to Alfred with the promise that they

Western Viking with heavy spear. (*Photo and copyright by Jomsborg Vikings Hird*)

Eastern Viking with fur cap. (*Photo and copyright by Jomsborg Vikings Hird*)

would immediatelyabandon the territory of Wessex. Three weeks after the Battle of Edington, Guthrum was baptized, with Alfred as his sponsor, and sometime later the Vikings abandoned Wessex and retreated to their bases in East Anglia, where they remained quiet for several years. A peace treaty was signed between the two parties, according to which Alfred was recognized by the Vikings as the overlord of the Saxons while the Scandinavian presence in England was acknowledged as a legitimate one by Alfred. This was the first fundamental step towards the formation of the Danelaw, the Viking state of eastern England.

In 879, new military reinforcements arrived from Scandinavia as a result of the Saxon victory at Edington. This new force was intent on resuming hostilities against Alfred, but Guthrum saw no reason to fight again, at least for the moment. The newly arrived Viking forces conducted some sporadic raids against the borders of Wessex, but Alfred repelled these quite easily thanks to the construction of new fortified positions known as 'burhs'. By 885, the internal divisions existing among the Vikings of England became deeper, with the newcomers settled in the northern portion of the Danelaw while Guthrum ruled East Anglia as a proper king who was recognized by Alfred the Great. The rulers of Wessex and East Anglia signed an important treaty in 886, which defined the border separating their two kingdoms. The Kingdom of Mercia was partitioned between Alfred and Guthrum: the western portion was given to Wessex, while the eastern one was given to East Anglia. During the last years of his rule, Alfred was able to expand his realm and reconquer (temporarily) York from the Vikings, while diplomatic relations between Wessex and East Anglia remained positive until his death in 899. Alfred had been able to stop the Vikings in their conquest of England and had unified under his rule all the Saxon territories that had not been conquered by the Scandinavians. By 900, the political situation of England had changed dramatically compared with that of the previous century. The Heptarchy was no longer in existence, since Wessex and the Danelaw controlled the whole of the country: East Anglia was in Viking hands, Mercia had been partitioned between Wessex and East Anglia, Northumbria was a Scandinavian protectorate, Essex was part of East Anglia, and Kent and Sussex were part of Wessex. Alfred the Great had been able to unify most of southern and eastern England, while the Vikings still controlled northern and western England.

After the death of Alfred, a civil war ravaged the newly unified Saxon kingdom, with two rivals fighting for the throne: Edward (elder son of Alfred) and Aethelwold (younger son of Aethelred). Aethelwold was the much weaker of the pretenders, since he could not count on the support of the most important Saxon aristocrats. As a result, Aethelwold decided to form a military alliance with the Vikings settled in Northumbria in order to secure the support of their warriors. The Saxon civil war came to an end in 903, when the Vikings of Northumbria were decisively defeated

Western Viking with Gjermundbu Helmet. (*Photo and copyright by Brokkar Lag*)

Eastern Viking with padded armour. (*Photo and copyright by Jomsborg Vikings Hird*)

by Edward after having ravaged most of Mercia. Aethelwold and his main Viking ally were killed in battle, and thus the elder son of Alfred the Great could finally consolidate his power. After some years of relative peace, hostilities between Edward and the Northumbrian Vikings resumed, leading to the Battle of Tettenhall in 910. This was a significant victory for the Saxons, who inflicted heavy losses on the Vikings before reconquering those areas of Mercia that had been lost.

While these events took place in England, the Scandinavians transformed Brittany in northern France into their main base on Continental Europe, and from there they started to launch destructive incursions against southern England. Edward repulsed these attacks and built a new defensive system based on forts across his realm. After defeating several Viking incursions from the sea and extending his political influence over southern Wales, the Saxon monarch resumed hostilities against the Danelaw with the objective of taking some border lands from East Anglia. During 917, thanks to a brilliant military campaign that was largely made up of sieges and counter-sieges, Edward was able to reduce the Viking presence in England in a major way. The whole central and southern portion of the Danelaw was taken by the Saxons, with the Vikings remaining in possession of only a few territories in Northumbria. Meanwhile, in Scandinavia, the political situation was changing very rapidly. The Danish Vikings, who had been the main driving force behind the victories of the Great Heathen Army, were gradually changing their lifestyle; a first form of centralized Danish kingdom was organized under the rule of Gorm the Old (ruled 936–958), while the Christian faith was introduced into the realm under the rule of Harald Bluetooth (958–986). As a result of these important changes, the number of Danish warriors willing to spend their life as seaborne raiders progressively decreased.

Chapter 4

The Viking Invasions of England

Around 918, a group of Norwegian Vikings, who had already been raiding in Ireland, conquered Northumbria from the Danes and occupied the city of York. As a result, the Danish presence in England came to an end, since both East Anglia and Essex had been taken by Edward a few years before. The Norwegian Vikings continued to control a significant portion of Northumbria for several decades, despite being constantly at war with the Saxon kingdom. The Scandinavian position in England, however, became increasingly precarious since the unified Saxons could deploy significant military resources in the field. The Vikings were expelled from York in 927; some years later, most of Northumbria was temporarily occupied by the Saxons. Around 940, however, the Vikings were able to reconquer part of their Northumbrian territories thanks to the decisive help of Scandinavian raiders based in Ireland and the arrival of new reinforcements from Norway. A new Viking war leader, Olaf of York, emerged and organized a major offensive against central England, with the objective of reconquering the territories of the former Danelaw. In 942, after some initial difficulties, the Saxons reorganized their military forces and repulsed the Viking offensive after retaking all the lands that had been occupied by the Scandinavians. The Viking realm in Northumbria survived for just another few years, the continuous wars with the Saxons and the revolts of the local population eventually causing its fall in 954. The Norwegian project of a Viking kingdom stretching from York to Dublin had failed; the last Scandinavian footholds in England had been destroyed after a century of Viking presence in the Saxon kingdoms.

The fall of the Danelaw and Northumbria, however, did not mark the end of the Viking raids in England: these continued during the following years, the Scandinavians never abandoning their ambition of conquering the country. The reign of the Saxon monarch Aethelred II (978–1013) saw a series of new Viking attacks against England, which took the form of raids but were conducted by significant numbers of warriors. In August 991, for example, a force of 4,000 Vikings commanded by Olaf Tryggvason disembarked at Maldon near the River Blackwater in Essex. The Scandinavians sailed up the river while the local Saxon forces organized themselves to face their threat. Byrhtnoth, Ealdorman of Essex, had a limited number of professional warriors under his command to stop the Vikings, and thus had no choice but to mobilize every able-bodied man in the region. The Scandinavians stopped at an island in the middle of the Blackwater and waited for the arrival of the enemy army. Initially, Tryggvason tried to find a compromise with the Saxons, promising that he would leave England if his invasion force was paid a large amount of gold. Byrhtnoth refused the offer and prepared his warriors for battle. A small land bridge connected the island occupied by the Vikings to the banks of the river, and thus the Saxons could defend this narrow passage with a limited number of men. The accounts that we have of the ensuing battle are not very precise, but what is known for sure is that the Scandinavians were able to move their main force to the banks of the river and to deploy it in combat formation. The subsequent fight was particularly violent, with many warriors killed on both sides, but despite suffering serious losses, the Vikings emerged victorious and the Saxons were completely routed. Byrhtnoth was among the Saxon casualties, together with several hundred of his men.

After the Battle of Maldon, the Viking force that had disembarked on the east coast of England could have easily raided deeply into the interior of England without encountering serious resistance. Aethelred II, unlike his predecessors, was a weak king with no great military capabilities. In addition, the arrival of a new Viking army in England had spread panic among the population, and it seemed that the resurgence of the Danelaw was imminent. Following the Saxon defeat at Maldon, the Archbishop of Canterbury, Sigeric, advised Aethelred to pay off the Vikings instead of trying to defeat them. Sigeric was supported in this by most of the Saxon warlords of south-eastern England, so the king had no choice but to agree to their requests and come to terms with the raiders. A danegeld tribute of 10,000 Roman pounds (3,300kg) of silver was paid to Olaf and his men, who left England after having raided the south-east for a short time.

The events of 991 showed the Vikings that the Saxon kingdom was too weak to repulse their attacks, and that a new invasion to conquer England was still possible. By simply appearing with their warships on the horizon, the Scandinavian warriors could terrorize the English population and force the Saxon authorities into paying the danegeld. Without even fighting, the Vikings could obtain enormous sums of gold and silver that would have taken many months of fighting to obtain. So although the Scandinavians no longer had a stable base in England, they still represented a deadly menace for the Saxon kingdom. During this period, the Vikings from Norway started to play a prominent role, since the 'first generation' of Danish raiders had by now changed their overall strategy. As mentioned above, an early form of a centralized Danish kingdom was developing in their homeland during these years, and an increasing number of Danish Vikings – especially those from the

Western Viking armed
with double-handed
Danish axe. (*Photo and
copyright by Brokkar Lag*)

Eastern Viking with spear and shield. (*Photo and copyright by Jomsborg Vikings Hird*)

Eastern Viking with fur cap. (*Photo and copyright by Brokkar Lag*)

Western Viking with fur cap and axe. (*Photo and copyright by Jomsborg Vikings Hird*)

southern regions of Jutland that bordered with Germany – were converting to the Christian faith. In Norway, however, the Vikings continued to live according to their traditional lifestyle and increased their raiding activities.

Meanwhile, the Scandinavians who had settled in Normandy, who will be covered in one of the next chapters, were gradually transforming themselves into feudal warlords and knights. Since 911, the Vikings of Normandy had become vassals of the Kingdom of France, with their territories organized as the Duchy of Normandy: they were becoming Normans and were gradually losing their original character of seaborne raiders. This 'feudalization' of the Normans had some very important practical consequences for the Vikings. Primarily, it led to the progressive disappearance of the Scandinavian naval bases in Normandy from which many raids against southern England had been launched. As a result, the new phase of Viking incursions and invasions that was opening would have a strong Norwegian character, since their most important new bases started to be located in the fiords of Norway. The Viking force that fought at the Battle of Maldon was the last one to attack England whose warriors were mostly from Denmark. It should be noted, however, that after the establishment of the Danish kingdom, the Vikings from this region continued to have ambitious plans regarding England. Differently from their Norwegian brethren, who were just interested in raiding or in being paid the danegeld, the Danish Vikings were starting to consider the possibility of a new permanent settlement in England. After being paid, Olaf Tryggvason was baptized a Christian, with Aethelred as his sponsor, and left the Saxon kingdom forever. Nevertheless, some of the warriors who had fought with him at Maldon decided to remain in England to serve as mercenaries, and were garrisoned on the Isle of Wight.

Aethelred II, however, had not resolved his problems with the Vikings. In 997, his Scandinavian mercenaries revolted and left the Isle of Wight to raid various nearby areas. Cornwall, Devon, Somerset and southern Wales were ravaged in 997; during the following year, the Vikings attacked Dorset, Hampshire and Sussex. In 999, the former mercenaries invested Kent, before being paid a second danelaw and leaving England for Normandy. During the following years, the Scandinavian raiders continued to frequently attack the Saxon kingdom, aided in doing so by having kept control of the Isle of Wight, which became their most important base. The weak Aethelred had no choice but to pay the Vikings with substantial amounts of gold and silver on many more occasions in order to save his kingdom, causing great malcontent among his subjects. At that time there were still substantial Scandinavian communities living in England in the former territories of the Danelaw. These were made up of peaceful individuals who had been loyal subjects of the Saxon kings for decades. The ethnic problems of the Saxon kingdom erupted in 1002, when

Aethelred II ordered the massacre of all the Scandinavians living in his realm. In what became known as 'Saint Brice's Day Massacre', thousands of former Vikings were slaughtered by the Saxons. Among the many victims of the massacre ordered by the Saxon king was Gunhilde, sister of Sweyn Forkbeard, the King of Denmark. In 1003, Forkbeard launched a massive invasion of eastern England to seek revenge for the many Scandinavian civilians who had been slaughtered during the previous year. He also wanted to create a new permanent settlement in the British Isles. The Danish Vikings raided East Anglia and sacked Norwich without meeting serious opposition. They later had to fight a pitched battle against a local warlord, from which they emerged victorious despite having suffered severe losses. In 1005, however, a severe famine afflicted the British Isles, causing Forkbeard's forces to experience serious logistical problems. To avoid the risk of losing his entire invading army from starvation, the Viking king finally decided to abandon England, having in the end obtained very little.

In 1009, a new Scandinavian invading force landed on the shores of the Saxon kingdom, commanded by the warlord Thorkell the Tall and comprising several thousand warriors. Initially, the Vikings marched towards Canterbury, but they were paid a large sum of money by the local community and thus did not invest the city. They then tried to take the city of London, but all their attempts were repulsed due to strong resistance by Saxon forces. In 1011, the Viking army returned to Canterbury and finally took it after a siege of three weeks, Archbishop Aelfheah being taken as a hostage by the raiders. Thorkell continued to terrorize southern England with his men for several months, until he was paid several times by the local communities, who offered him the danegeld in order to save their lives and homes. In total, some 48,000 pounds of silver were given to the Vikings before they left England during 1012. Like several other Scandinavian leaders before him, Thorkell decided to remain in the Saxon kingdom with some of his most trusted men in order to serve as mercenaries for Aethelred II.

In 1013, the Vikings of Denmark mounted a new large-scale invasion against England, led by Sweyn Forkbeard and his son Cnut (the future 'Cnut the Great'). The Scandinavian army landed at Sandwich and soon assumed control over most of East Anglia before moving to Northumbria. There was still a significant number of Scandinavians in Northumbria, who had not been affected by the massacre of 1002 and who now welcomed the Danish warriors. Sweyn and Cnut seemed unstoppable, Aethelred proving too slow in organizing an effective military response. They conquered the five main cities of the former Danelaw, which were collectively known as the 'Five Boroughs': Derby, Leicester, Lincoln, Nottingham and Stamford. After crossing Watling Street, which was one of the most important land routes of Saxon

Western Viking
equipped with sword
and shield. (*Photo and
copyright by Jomsborg
Vikings Hird*)

Western Viking with chainmail and spear. (*Photo and copyright by Jomsborg Vikings Hird*)

England, the Danish monarch advanced on Oxford and Winchester before moving against London. By now it was clear that the Vikings wanted to assume control over the whole Saxon kingdom, and thus the destiny of England was in their hands. Aethelred II and Thorkell reorganized their forces and put up a strong resistance against the invaders around London. In the end, however, the Vikings were able to prevail, as they by then controlled all the kingdom apart from the Saxon capital. Aethelred understood that further resistance would have been pointless, and thus fled to the Isle of Wight before leaving his kingdom in exile. On Christmas Day 1013, Sweyn Forkbeard was proclaimed King of England: the Vikings had finally turned their dream of conquering the Saxon kingdom into reality. A few weeks after these events, however, Sweyn died and a major revolt broke out among the Saxons (who had never accepted foreign rule). Upon the king's death, his older son, Harald, was proclaimed King of Denmark, while his younger son, Cnut, was made King of England. Cnut, however, was unable to rule his new realm because Aethelred returned from exile and the whole Saxon population revolted against him. Cnut had no choice but to flee England in order to save his life, Aethelred having formed a strong military alliance with the Norwegian warlord Olaf Haraldsson. The Saxon king was able to reconquer his realm with the help of his new Norwegian allies, but when the latter left England, he had to face a major revolt organized by his son and future successor, Edmund Ironside. The outbreak of this civil war in the Saxon kingdom offered a great opportunity to Cnut, who quickly organized his own reconquest of England.

Chapter 5

The Conquests of Cnut the Great

In the summer of 1015, while the civil war between Aethelred and Edmund was reaching its peak, Cnut landed on the English coastline at the head of a massive Viking army recruited from every corner of Scandinavia. According to modern estimates, Cnut the Great commanded a total of 10,000 warriors who were transported in 200 warships. This time the Vikings landed in Wessex, to menace the very heart of the Saxon kingdom. The Scandinavians landed without meeting any serious opposition, raiding several settlements. Although Wessex was still under the control of Aethelred, he had been severely weakened by the rebellion of his son. When Eadric Streona, the Ealdorman of Mercia, changed sides and joined the invaders, it became apparent that the old Saxon monarch could not continue his resistance for long. Thorkell the Tall also abandoned Aethelred and joined Cnut, before the Vikings crossed the Thames and attacked Warwickshire. Edmund Ironside tried to stop the invaders on several occasions, but was unable to achieve significant results since the area surrounding London was still loyal to his father. Understanding that the only way to slow down the enemy was to combine their forces, Aethelred and Edmund temporarily put aside their differences, but still achieved very little. Cnut occupied Northumbria and continued to enlarge the ranks of his troops by recruiting dissident Saxon aristocrats who were opposed to the old king and his son.

On 23 April 1016, Aethelred died after many years of rule and was succeeded by his son, Edmund. But although Edmund was now the only supreme ruler of the Saxons, this did not change the military situation. The new monarch remained in London for several months, since his troops were in no condition to conduct offensive operations. The Saxon capital was well defended with thick wooden walls and had substantial food reserves, so Edmund hoped that a long and successful resistance would be possible. When the Scandinavians surrounded London, however, the Saxon king changed his mind and moved to Wessex in order to raise a new army there. Cnut divided his army into two parts: one remained around London to blockade the city, while the other went to Wessex with the objective of chasing down Edmund. The siege of the Saxon capital was a difficult operation for the Vikings, who constructed dikes on the flanks of the city and dug a channel across the banks of the Thames in order to cut communications up-river for the besieged. Meanwhile, Edmund was able to raise a substantial military force in Wessex and fought two minor battles against the Scandinavian army that was on his tracks. These actions, which took place in Somerset and Wiltshire, proved indecisive. The Saxons were able to continue their march towards London and to relieve the city from its siege after crossing the Thames at Brentford. This victory, however, was short-lived, since Edmund soon had to march back to Wessex in order to replenish his losses. London was besieged again by Cnut, but once again the Vikings could not take the city. This was a crucial phase of the conflict, since both sides were by now exhausted. Eadric Streona then decided to change sides and abandoned Cnut, while the latter ravaged Mercia in search of a decisive victory.

In October 1016, the decisive battle for the destiny of England was fought at Assandon, in north-west Essex. Both Edmund and Cnut employed their best troops in the clash, whose outcome was decided by Eadric Streona, who once again changed sides during the battle and gave victory to the Vikings of Cnut. Edmund, soundly defeated, fled westwards to Gloucestershire. Although he could count on the support there of several Welsh nobles, he was defeated again by the pursuing Vikings during a minor clash. After being wounded and having lost most of his supporters, the Saxon king had no choice but to come to terms with the invaders. A peace treaty was signed between him and Cnut, according to which England would be divided into two parts: all the lands located north of the Thames would be ruled by Cnut, with all those to the south (including London) ruled by Edmund. Upon Edmund's death, Cnut would rule the whole of England. Just a few weeks after the signing of the treaty, Edmund Ironside died from wounds suffered in battle, and thus Cnut the Great could be crowned as the sole ruler of England.

In 1017, after decades of attempts and failures, the Vikings had finally completed their conquest of the English kingdom. Cnut ruled England for almost two decades and proved to be one of the nation's most successful kings. His rise to power halted Scandinavian raids for a long period, heralding an age of prosperity for the Saxon population. In 1018, after collecting a colossal danegeld from his new kingdom, Cnut paid all his warriors and sent most of them back home in order to preserve the internal stability of England. Only forty Viking warships remained in England with their crews, becoming a sort of standing army that was paid with a special new tax that was introduced by Cnut (known as 'heregeld', or 'army payment'). The new king reorganized England from an administrative point of view, dividing the territory of his realm into four parts: Wessex was kept under his personal control, while Northumbria was assigned to Erik of Hlathir, East Anglia was given to Thorkell the Tall and Mercia remained in the hands of Eadric Streona. Over time, Cnut substituted his loyal Scandinavian followers with Saxon nobles he trusted, which helped him in gaining the support of much of the population.

While the events described above took place in England, the political situation in Scandinavia changed dramatically. Olaf Haraldsson, after returning to his homeland,

Eastern Viking with Gjermundbu Helmet having aventail of mail. (*Photo and copyright by Jomsborg Vikings Hird*)

Western Viking with helmet and chainmail. (*Photo and copyright by Sjórvaldar Vikings*)

Eastern Viking equipped with spear and shield. (*Photo and copyright by Jomsborg Vikings Hird*)

Eastern Viking with Gjermundbu Helmet and loose trousers. (*Photo and copyright by Jomsborg Vikings Hird*)

had been able to free Norway from the influence of Denmark by winning the Battle of Nesjar in 1016, and had thus started to organize a first 'structured' Kingdom of Norway. In 1018, Cnut's brother and King of Denmark, Harald, died; this event, together with the ascendancy of Olaf Haraldsson, opened a new phase in Scandinavian history. After the sudden death of Harald II, Cnut the Great went to Denmark at the head of a fleet to claim the Danish throne. After fighting several minor clashes against local opponents, he was finally crowned as King of Denmark and returned to England in 1020. A vast 'Viking Empire' was thus born in Northern Europe, which comprised England as well as Denmark. The empire was guided by the greatest warlord of the time, who still had expansionist ambitions. Indeed, Cnut had plans for dominating the whole Scandinavian world, and had plans to attack the Vikings of Norway and Sweden. By this time, Norway and Sweden were already organized as two semi-centralized kingdoms: the first, as we have seen, was led by Olaf Haraldsson, while the second was guided by Anund Jacob. The two kings feared that Cnut the Great could defeat them in detail by using his superior military resources, and thus decided to put aside the differences existing between them in order to form an alliance. They started to launch a series of attacks against Denmark and incited the local regent to revolt against Cnut. During 1026, in order to restore his power in Scandinavia, Cnut assembled a large fleet of English and Danish warships and attacked the naval forces of his two enemies. A large battle was fought at Helgea, off the coast of Sweden, which saw the triumph of Cnut the Great: the Norwegian and Swedish Vikings suffered a decisive defeat. In 1028, after travelling to Rome and securing his position in England, Cnut the Great decided to bring Norway back under the influence of Denmark, and thus sailed against Olaf Haraldsson at the head of a fleet. Haraldsson was unable to put up any effective resistance because the most important Norwegian warlords revolted against him. He had no choice but to surrender. As a result, Cnut could now add the Kingdom of Norway to his personal possessions. In 1030, Olaf Haraldsson tried to reconquer his former realm at the head of a Swedish army, but he was defeated and killed by the Norwegians at the Battle of Stiklestad.

Cnut the Great died in 1035, after having ruled a vast portion of Northern Europe for several years. In Denmark, he was succeeded by his son Harthacnut, who soon had to face a Norwegian rebellion. The Norwegians were able to restore the independence of their kingdom under the leadership of Magnus Haraldsson (son of Olaf Haraldsson). In England, Cnut was succeeded by his other son, Harold Harefoot, who was to rule there on behalf of Harthacnut while the latter was in Denmark. However, Harold Harefoot decided to claim the English throne for himself in 1037, and rebelled against his brother. The reign of Harold Harefoot continued until he died in 1040, when Harthacnut was finally able to stabilize his position in Scandinavia and return to England to claim his throne.

Chapter 6

Harald Hardrada and the Battle of Stamford Bridge

Denmark and England were ruled by Harthacnut until his death in 1042, after which both countries entered into a very chaotic political phase. Control of Denmark was contested between a local pretender named Sweyn Estridsson and the Norwegian monarch Magnus Haraldsson. The hostilities came to a definitive end only in 1046, when Magnus died and Sweyn could remain as the sole ruler of Denmark. In England, the death of Harthacnut was followed by the re-emergence of the Saxon 'House of Wessex', with Edward the Confessor, son of Aethelred II, proclaimed as king. Edward had spent most of his life as an exile in Normandy, and thus, after his ascendancy to the throne, the Normans started to exert an increasing political influence over the English court. Edward the Confessor died without direct heirs on 5 January 1066, causing the beginning of the worst dynastical crisis endured by England during the central centuries of the Middle Ages. No less than four different pretenders claimed their right to sit on the English throne. The first was Edgar Aetheling, who was just 15 in 1066 and was the grandson of Edmund Ironside. The second claimant was Harold Godwinson, Earl of Wessex, who was Edward the Confessor's brother-in-law but who had no blood connection with the recent king. The third was Harald Hardrada, successor of Magnus Haraldsson and King of Norway since 1046, who had no blood ties with Edward the Confessor. The final pretender was William, Duke of Normandy since 1035, who was a cousin of the king through Edward's mother, Emma (who was William's great-aunt). Edward the Confessor had promised his throne to both William and Harold during two different phases of his long life, and this caused great confusion. The weakest of the pretenders was Edgar Aetheling, who was the only one who could not count on an army to support his claim. Harald Hardrada was a true Viking and had strong military forces, but his claims on the English throne were weak from a dynastic point of view; he had already tried to become King of Denmark in 1064, but his attempt had failed. He decided to invade England after concluding an important alliance with Tostig Godwinson, who revolted against his brother Harold Godwinson after the latter was proclaimed King of England in 1066. From a political point of view, Harald Hardrada's landing on English shores would have been perceived by the local Saxon population as just another Viking invasion. Nevertheless, the Norwegian warlord had

Western Viking with hood and chainmail. (*Photo and copyright by Sjórvaldar Vikings*)

Eastern Viking with chainmail and axe. (*Photo and copyright by Jomsborg Vikings Hird*)

a good chance of victory, since England was invaded simultaneously by two armies in 1066, so Harold Godwinson would have been obliged to divide his military forces into two parts. The Saxon leader could count on the support of the most prominent nobles of his country, who were against the possibility of choosing a foreign king like the Norman William or the Norwegian Harald.

After Edward the Confessor's death, the Saxon nobles elected Harold as their king very rapidly in order to gain some time in view of upcoming military events: they knew very well that a Norman army and a Viking one were about to attack their country. After hearing of Harold Godwinson's coronation, William of Normandy started assembling a massive fleet in order to transport his military forces to England. He could count on the support of the English Church and of some nobles, who were against Harold's political plans. The new Saxon king prepared himself to face the Normans and recruited a large army that comprised a significant number of professional warriors. The Saxons deployed themselves on the Isle of Wight and waited for the arrival of the Normans. The latter, however, were blocked in their ports for seven months due to unfavourable weather conditions, and thus William could not conduct his invasion with the planned timing. This delay also caused significant problems for Harold, since his plan was to defeat the Normans before facing the second invasion led by Harald Hardrada. The Saxon king knew that the Vikings would need several months to assemble a sizeable invasion force, unlike the Normans who were already ready and would have been able to attack in a few weeks. The delay of seven months suffered by William meant that the two invasions would take place at exactly the same time. Harold knew that the Normans would land in southern England, but had no idea where the Vikings would attack his country. It was presumed that Harald Hardrada's target would have been East Anglia or Northumbria.

The Vikings, sailing from Norway, landed on 8 September 1066 at the mouth of the River Tyne, having Northumbria as their first target. As anticipated above, Harald Hardrada counted on the support of Tostig Godwinson, who had revolted against his brother Harold and had already tried to form an alliance with William of Normandy. When William refused his offer, Tostig went to the King of Norway and decided to join him in his invasion of England. The brother of the Saxon monarch proved to be a precious ally for Harald, since he knew the terrain on which the Vikings were going to operate and he was in contact with several of the most important Saxon nobles of northern England. After joining his forces with those of Tostig, Harald sailed along the River Ouse towards York. This city had long been the most important land base of the Vikings in England, and its capture would have been vital for the Scandinavian invasion force. Harold Godwinson had entrusted the defence of the northern part of his kingdom to the two most powerful warlords of the area: the brothers Edwin, Earl of Mercia, and Morcar, Earl of Northumbria. They had already mobilized part of their military forces in view of the Viking invasion, and were able to move against Harald in order to prevent the fall of York. On 20 September, not far from York, they fought against the Scandinavians at the Battle of Fulford. The Viking army numbered some 10,000 men, while the Saxons were in clear numerical inferiority, having assembled just 4,500 warriors (3,000 from Northumbria and 1,500 from Mercia). Edwin and Morcar, however, could deploy their forces in a very good defensive position that had the River Ouse on the right flank and a swampy area known as the 'Fordland' on the left flank. Harald deployed his forces on higher ground, but could not conduct a manoeuvre of encirclement on the wings of his enemy. At the beginning of the clash, the Saxons made a major mistake: instead of remaining in their defensive positions, they decided to launch a frontal attack against the Vikings. The Saxon offensive took place while the Scandinavians were still completing the deployment of their troops, but was a complete failure. Harald soon organized a counter-attack with his best warriors, forcing the Saxons to give ground. The decisive moment of the battle came when, against all odds, the Vikings were able to cross the River Ouse on one side and the Fordland on the other in order to attack the Saxons from three sides. Outnumbered and outmanoeuvred, the warriors of Edwin and Morcar had no choice but to flee from the battlefield. With York occupied by the Vikings soon after their victory, it became clear that northern England was now vulnerable to conquest by Harald Hardrada.

When news of the Fulford defeat reached Harold Godwinson, the Saxon monarch was shocked but reacted very rapidly: he determined to force-march his royal army 190 miles north from London to York in order to prevent the loss of the northern part of his kingdom. Harold's position as a great military leader was confirmed by the fact that less than a week after hearing of the Battle of Fulford, his forces were already facing Harald Hardrada around York. The Saxon warriors who arrived in the northern theatre of operations were extremely tired, since they had marched day and night for a week, but they were more numerous than their opponents. According to modern estimates, the Vikings had lost 1,000 men at Fulford, and thus fielded 9,000 fighters in total, while Harold had mustered 10,000 infantrymen and 2,000 cavalrymen. The Scandinavians were taken by surprise, having not imagined that the Saxon royal army could reach York in such a short time. The decisive clash of Harald Hardrada's invasion of England then took place at Stamford Bridge, on the River Derwent. When the battle began, some of the Viking forces were on the western bank of the river, but the majority were on the eastern bank as they had no idea that the Saxons where moving towards their positions. Caught by surprise, the Vikings on the eastern bank of the Derwent decided to deploy themselves into a defensive circle formation.

Western Viking with helmet having nasal. (*Photo and copyright by Jomsborg Vikings Hird*)

Western Viking warlord with standard and horn. (*Photo and copyright by Sjórvaldar Vikings*)

Those on the western bank, however, were rapidly massacred by the Saxons, with just a handful of them able to escape by crossing the bridge that gave the battle its name. At this point of the clash, Harold had to face a serious problem, his troops having no choice but to pass through the choke-point represented by the bridge in order to attack the Vikings. According to contemporary sources, a single giant warrior from the army of Harald Hardrada (armed with a massive two-handed axe) blocked the narrow crossing and repulsed the Saxon warriors alone for some time. He killed forty enemies before a Saxon warrior floated under the bridge and thrust his spear through its planks in order to mortally wound the giant axeman. After pouring across to the eastern bank of the Derwent, the Saxons deployed in battle line just short of the Viking circle. They then locked their shields and charged against the defensive formation of the enemy. The ensuing phase of the battle, characterized by harsh hand-to-hand fighting, lasted for several hours, during which the Scandinavians resisted with great determination. Both sides suffered heavy losses and the outcome of the clash was in the balance. Harald Hardrada fought with great courage among his elite warriors, and tried to resist for as long as possible. At a certain point, however, the defensive formation of the Viking army began to fragment and its initial cohesion was lost. The Saxons were finally able to break the enemy wall of shields at several points and gradually started to surround isolated groups of Scandinavians. When it became clear that his army was in the process of being outflanked, Harald Hardrada did not attempt to abandon the battlefield but instead continued to fight at the head of his remaining warriors. He was killed by an enemy arrow, at which his remaining army dissolved in chaos. During this final phase of the clash, which saw the rout of the Viking army, Tostig Godwinson was also killed. Just when everything seemed lost for the Scandinavians, some Viking reinforcements arrived on the battlefield; these consisted of warriors who had been left behind by Harald in order to guard his warships, who were under the command of his prospective son-in-law, Eystein Orre. The latter launched a violent counter-attack against the Saxons, but this was easily repulsed by Harold's men, with Eystein being killed during the fighting. After several hours of intense combat, Harald Hardrada's Viking army had been completely wiped out. According to contemporary sources, so many Saxons and Norwegians died at Stamford Bridge that the battlefield upon which the clash took place was still whitened with bleached bones fifty years after 1066.

After obtaining such a brilliant victory, Harold Godwinson concluded a truce with the surviving Vikings, who were allowed to leave England after giving pledges not to attack the Saxon kingdom again. The losses of the Scandinavians were so severe that just twenty-four of their warships returned home to Norway. Although Harold had destroyed the military forces of one of his rivals, the losses for his army had been substantial. Then, just three days after the Battle of Stamford Bridge, on 28 September, William and his Normans landed in southern England at Pevensey Bay in Sussex. Without having time to replenish his losses or reorganize his troops, Harold had to march south very rapidly at the head of his exhausted warriors. For the second time in a few days, the Saxon army had to cover an immense distance in just a few days. When they arrived in the south to intercept the Normans, they were very tired but their morale was extremely high. Three weeks after Stamford Bridge, at the Battle of Hastings, the Saxons were defeated decisively by the Normans and Harold Godwinson was killed by an enemy arrow. The glorious centuries of Saxon England had finally come to an end, and William the Conqueror could be crowned as the heir of Edward the Confessor. From a military point of view, the Battle of Stamford Bridge was a key factor behind the Norman victory at Hastings. If the Saxons had faced the Normans before fighting against the Vikings, the former would have had serious difficulties in breaking Harold's defences in southern England.

The events of 1066 marked a real turning point, not only in the history of England but also in that of the Vikings. After being defeated at Stamford Bridge, the Scandinavians finally abandoned their dreams of conquering the British Isles. During the following decades, however, the Vikings continued to attack England for different reasons, and thus the menace represented by them did not disappear completely. In 1070, Sweyn Estridsson, King of Denmark, decided to give his support to the last pretender to the English throne who had not been already eliminated by William the Conqueror: the Saxon noble Edgar Aetheling. The Danish fleet sent to support Edgar attacked Northumbria and was able to capture York, since the Normans had not yet secured their occupation of England. In order to avoid the outbreak of a civil war inside his new realm and the beginning of a difficult conflict with Sweyn Estridsson, King William decided to come to terms with the Danes and paid them a large sum of money. The Vikings thus left northern England and abandoned Edgar Aetheling to his destiny. However, in 1075, Sweyn Estridsson's sons sailed to the Norman kingdom at the head of a fleet in order to support a Saxon rebellion that was ravaging England. But when this new Viking expedition arrived, the revolt had already been suppressed by William, so the Scandinavians went back home without achieving anything. They had plundered the city of York and some surrounding areas, but returned to their ships before facing any Norman counter-offensive. The final major attempted Viking intervention was in 1085, when Sweyn Estridsson's son and heir, Cnut IV, planned a new invasion of England, but he was never able to assemble a sizeable fleet to start such an operation. The bloody days of the Viking invasions were over for the British Isles, the Normans having established a strong and centralized feudal monarchy in their new realm. The Scandinavians continued to

Eastern Viking with fur cap and kaftan.
(*Photo and copyright by Brokkar Lag*)

Western Viking with helmet having nasal. (*Photo and copyright by Jomsborg Vikings Hird*)

launch minor raids against England after 1085, but these were just sporadic attacks that were conducted by a limited number of warships. Later, during the period commonly known as 'The Anarchy' (1135–1153), the Norwegians took advantage of the ongoing civil war between Stephen of Blois and Henry Plantagenet to plunder the eastern coast of England. By this time, however, the Scandinavians attacking the British Isles were no longer Vikings, but 'Norwegians' in the modern sense of the word. They had no intention of conquering any territory in England, simply wanting to plunder as much as possible. With the ascendancy of the Plantagenets, these occasional and short-lived raids ceased forever.

Chapter 7

The Vikings in Wales and Scotland

Wales, due to its geographical position, was not attacked by the Vikings with the same degree of violence and continuity that was experienced by England. During the early phase of the Scandinavian raids in the British Isles, the Vikings created some short-lived temporary settlements in Pembrokeshire and on the Gower Peninsula. The raiders, however, were not able to establish a significant presence due to the strong resistance of the local aristocrats and the lack of rivers that could be employed by them as navigable waterways. During the ninth century, Wales was strongly linked to the Celtic communities who lived in the French region of Brittany, which came under a strong Scandinavian influence in that period. After settling in Normandy, the Vikings established a solid alliance with the aristocrats of Brittany. This had positive consequences for the Welsh princes, who exchanged goods with the French Britons and had strong cultural links with them. With the arrival of the Great Heathen Army and the ascendancy of Alfred the Great, however, relations between the Welsh and Vikings changed somewhat. In 893, a force of 250 Scandinavian warships appeared off the coast of the Lympne estuary in Kent and disembarked a large Viking army which built a strong fortified position at Appledore. The invaders brought their wives and children with them, since they intended to create a permanent settlement. Alfred the Great did not attack the invaders immediately, since he needed more time to gather his military resources. During the following weeks, the Vikings received some significant reinforcements and resumed their advance from their base at Appledore. Alfred sent part of his troops, under command of his son Edward, to stop the Scandinavians; a battle was fought at Farnham, in modern Surrey, which resulted in a victory for the Saxons. The Vikings were later defeated for a second time, after which they decided to join their forces with another group of Scandinavians based at Shoebury in Essex.

Hostilities continued between the Vikings and Saxons for several months, largely because Alfred was heavily involved against other Scandinavian forces that were attacking other areas of England. The English monarch and his son were eventually able to assemble a sizeable army in order to defeat the Essex-based Vikings once and for all. Alfred's army comprised a significant number of Welsh warriors, who had decided to join forces with the Saxons in order to eliminate a Scandinavian presence that represented a great potential threat to their lands. The combined Saxon and Welsh army attacked the Vikings and forced them to move to the north-west, where the Scandinavians were besieged at Buttington. The Vikings were blockaded in this town for several weeks, with many of them dying of hunger. The few survivors had no option but to surrender, giving the Saxons and Welsh an important victory. After being defeated at Buttington, the Vikings no longer represented a danger for Wales, where their raids became very sporadic. In 903, a group of Vikings from Dublin occupied the island of Anglesey, intending to establish a permanent foothold in Wales. This early attempt at colonizing Anglesey failed, but was followed by several further Scandinavian raids against the island. Around 1000, a Viking stronghold was built on Anglesey, but this proved short-lived. Cornwall, located south of Wales and having a lot in common with the Welsh from a cultural point of view, was occasionally attacked by the Vikings from 833 onwards. Between 1001 and 1003, the Scandinavians occupied the city of Exeter, but they were then expelled from the region.

If the Viking presence in Wales was never a significant one, the same could not be said for the other two Celtic nations of the British Isles: Scotland and Ireland. The Viking presence in Scotland began with occasional raids that were launched against important religious sites, starting in 794. The monastery of Iona, the most important religious site in Scotland, was twice assaulted by the Scandinavians, in 802 and 806. During the following decades, the intensity of Viking raids grew, with large fleets of their warships starting to appear off the coast of Scotland. As mentioned above, the Scottish lands were divided into three main realms during the early ninth century: the large Kingdom of Fortriu, the Kingdom of Dál Riata and the Kingdom of Strathclyde. Fortriu, populated by the warlike Picts, was the dominant military power in Scotland and was frequently at war with the other two kingdoms. Dál Riata was inhabited by the Scoti, who controlled the whole territory of Ireland, while Strathclyde was populated by Britons, who had a lot in common with the Welsh communities to the south. In 839, a large Viking army landed in Scotland to conduct a major incursion. To face this unexpected threat, the Kingdoms of Fortriu and Dál Riata formed an alliance and joined their military forces to meet the Scandinavians. In what was the first major campaign fought in Scotland against the Vikings, the local warriors were utterly defeated in a bloody battle of which we know very little. The kings of Fortriu and of Dál Riata were both killed during this clash.

As the years passed by, the Vikings conquered all the islands located around Britain, from the Isle of Man to the Shetland Islands. These new possessions formed an 'empire of the isles' and were used as important naval bases to conduct raids against the Scottish coastline. Moving from the Orkney and Shetland Islands the Scandinavians

Eastern Viking
warlord with double-
handed Danish axe.
(*Photo and copyright by
Sjórvaldar Vikings*)

Western Viking equipped with sword and shield. (*Photo and copyright by Jomsborg Vikings Hird*)

attacked the northern areas of the Highlands, notably Caithness and Sutherland. The latter were inhabited by the Picts of the Cat tribe, one of the most warlike communities of the Kingdom of Fortriu who enjoyed a certain degree of autonomy. Guided by experienced warlords such as Sigurd Eysteinsson and Thorstein the Red, the Vikings conquered Caithness and Sutherland before turning their attention to the southern areas of Ross and Moray (which were never fully conquered by them). The resistance of the local Picts was courageous but desperate, since they were quite isolated from the rest of the Kingdom of Fortriu, while the Scandinavians could rely on supplies from their bases in the northern islands. The Viking territories of northern Scotland were unified in a single political entity, which gradually lost its original 'piratical' nature when the frequency of Scandinavian incursions decreased. This area of the Highlands would continue to have a distinct Scandinavian character for the following two centuries, albeit politically being part of the Kingdom of Scotland. As we have seen, the Northern Isles (Orkney and Shetland) were the main bases from which the Vikings attacked the northern portion of the Highlands. Meanwhile, the western part of the Highlands became the target of Vikings from the Outer and Inner Hebrides. Differently from what happened in Caithness and Sutherland, however, the Scandinavians never established a permanent presence in the western Highlands, since they conducted raids only to capture slaves or occupy coastal areas on a temporary basis. The Viking lands of northern Scotland were collectively known as Lothlend or Lochlainn, and were colonized from the beginning by Norwegian warriors. Initially, these fighters were under direct control of their homeland, but over time they created their own independent dynasty and started to be strongly linked with the Vikings of Ireland.

The Scandinavian presence in the Highlands had important consequences for the political situation of Scotland, being an indirect but fundamental factor behind the unification of Fortriu and Dál Riata into a single realm. Around 843, Kenneth MacAlpin became king of the Picts as well as of the Scoti from western Scotland. A new dynasty, known as the House of Alpin, was born and a first form of an organized 'Kingdom of Scotland' (known as the Kingdom of Alba from 900) started to emerge. After the unification of Fortriu and Dál Riata, the Kingdom of Strathclyde became the main target of the Viking raids in Scotland. In 870, a large Scandinavian force from Ireland laid siege for four months to Alt Cnut. The campaign culminated in a victory for the Vikings, who were also able to capture the king of Strathclyde. The Britons of western Scotland slowly lost most of their military capabilities due to the frequent Scandinavian raids, and thus their kingdom became increasingly subordinate to that of the Saxons or to the Kingdom of Alba. In 937, the Saxons defeated the Britons of Strathclyde at the Battle of Brunanburh and installed a puppet king in

Eastern Viking
with fur cap and
Gjermundbu Helmet.
(*Photo and copyright
by Confraternita del
Leone/Historia Viva*)

Eastern Viking with kaftan and spear. (*Photo and copyright by Jomsborg Vikings Hird*)

western Scotland. Some decades later, when the Saxons experienced very difficult times due to Viking invasions, the Kingdom of Alba took advantage of the situation to invade and annex the Kingdom of Strathclyde around 1030.

Despite being quite strong from a military point of view, especially after their unification, the Picts and Scots experienced great difficulties in containing Viking raids. After the Scandinavians established a permanent base in Dublin and occupied Northumbria, the new realm created by Kenneth MacAlpin was surrounded by hostile communities. In 875, at the Battle of Dollar, the Picts and Scots were decisively defeated by a Viking army and suffered heavy casualties. After this clash, large portions of Scotland were raided by the Scandinavians, who met no serious opposition. From 900, however, the general situation started to improve for the Picts and Scots with the gradual emergence of the more centralized and gaelicized Kingdom of Alba. The new realm was the result of a fusion between the different cultures of the Picts and the Scots; the former represented the majority of the new kingdom's population, while the latter extended their Gaelic culture to most of Scotland (we could say that the Picts were 'gaelicized'). In 902, the Vikings lost their vital base of Dublin, which helped the Kingdom of Alba exert stronger control over its western coastline. For Scotland, the tenth century was full of battles fought against the Scandinavians, with the Kingdom of Alba emerging as the victor on several occasions. The Scots obtained a clear success over the Vikings in 962 at the Battle of Bauds after which the Scandinavians ceased to represent a menace for mainland Scotland, henceforth ruling only the area of Lochlainn. After the ascendancy of the Kingdom of Alba, the Scandinavians of Caithness and Sutherland were forced to deal with the Scots on almost equal terms. After having been autonomous for several decades, the Vikings of Lochlainn had returned to being under the influence of Norway by 1000 and were ruled by the Earldom of Orkney (a fiefdom of the Norwegians). In 1196, Harald Maddadsson, Earl of Orkney, agreed to become a fief of the Kingdom of Alba and started to pay a monetary tribute to William I of Scotland for possession of Caithness and Sutherland. Subsequently, the Scandinavians living in mainland Scotland were gradually absorbed into the local population.

Chapter 8

The Vikings in Ireland and the Battle of Clontarf

The first recorded Viking raid in Irish history took place in 795, when a small group of Scandinavians, presumably coming from Norway, looted the small island of Lambay not far from Dublin. Some years later, the pirates returned to conduct further devastating attacks in the same area and along the coastline of Connacht. Like those that took place in England and Scotland during this same period, these early raids shocked the local communities but did not cause major changes in the affected areas. The early Viking raiders were only in search of treasures to plunder and slaves to capture. Nevertheless, the appearance of the Scandinavians marked the beginning of a new phase in the history of Ireland: the 'golden age' that had seen the Scoti/Gaels convert to the Christian faith came to an end, replaced by a new period characterized by violence and terror. The Vikings slowly intensified their attacks against Ireland while continuing to have as their main targets the most important religious sites of the island. Similarly to what happened in Scotland, they initiated their permanent colonization by conquering some minor islands located around Ireland; the Skelling Islands soon became an important naval base for the Scandinavians. When the menace represented by the Vikings intensified, the nobles who dominated the Irish political scene were unable to organize an effective response. At that time, as we have seen, the territory of the island was fragmented into several small kingdoms that were constantly at war against each other. There was a very strong rivalry, for example, between the Kingdom of Munster in the south-west and that of Leinster in the south-east. The Scandinavians used these internal divisions of the Irish realms to their advantage and thus started planning a permanent settlement in Ireland. As the decades passed by, especially from 820 onwards, the Vikings started to create fortified encampments (known as 'longports') along the Irish coastline; here they spent the winter months, when the climatic conditions did not permit them to conduct raids. The fact that the Vikings preferred remaining in Ireland during the winter instead of returning home indicates that they felt absolutely safe in Irish lands and that the Irish opposition to their penetration was very weak. The most important of the longports was established on the River Liffey and was named Duiblinn, which would later become the largest Viking base in the British Isles and the first nucleus of present-day Dublin.

After securing their positions on the coast, the Scandinavians began using the major rivers of Ireland to conduct long-range raids inland. These were particularly devastating and involved hundreds of warriors, their usual targets being monastic settlements like those at Armagh, Glendalough, Kildare, Slane, Clonard, Clonmacnoise and Lismore. The Vikings' many victories obliged the Irish kings to modify their usual political attitude, since unity was the only factor that could enable them to stop the raids. In 848, the Kingdoms of Munster and Leinster joined together their military forces to face a large Scandinavian army that had landed in Ireland. The Irish warriors were able to achieve a significant victory over the Vikings, but were only able to get them to suspend their incursions for a short period. After 848, the Scandinavians adopted a new strategy of penetration in Ireland: instead of fighting against all the kingdoms at the same time, they formed local alliances with some and offered their services as mercenaries to the nobles who were involved in Irish internal conflicts. Two Viking warlords, named Olaf and Ivar, were particularly active in Ireland during this period. They concluded alliances with several Irish kings and changed sides according to circumstances. Thanks to their superior military capabilities, the Scandinavians could determine the outcome of a local conflict and thus were particularly appreciated as mercenaries by the Irish warlords. Occasionally, one of the Irish leaders was able to annex other kingdoms to his realm and thus assume the title of 'High King', yet this was little more than an honorific title since just about every attempt at political unification ended in failure.

While the Irish aristocrats killed each other in futile and interminable wars, the Vikings operating from Dublin increased their power. Generally speaking, the opposition to them was stronger in northern Ireland, since the southern part of the island was exhausted by the frequent clashes between Munster and Leinster. Around 873, however, the Vikings of Ireland experienced a period of crisis, with both Olaf and Ivar dying and an internal conflict breaking out to determine their successors, which had negative consequences for the system of the longports. The Irish rulers took advantage of the temporary Scandinavian weakness to organize a joint attack against the Viking base of Dublin, which was captured in 902, a year that saw the Scandinavians experiencing serious military difficulties. The Vikings were expelled from Ireland for several years, but two new fleets from Norway appeared off the Irish coast in 914: the first, guided by Ragnall, disembarked its warriors at Waterford, while the second, commanded by Sitric, landed near Leixlip. The Irish assembled two armies to stop the Vikings. One attacked Ragnall in Munster, but was unable to engage the Scandinavians in a decisive battle; the other moved against Sitric in Leinster and was utterly defeated at the Battle of Confey. Following their victories, the Vikings resumed their advance and reconquered Dublin. Ragnall left Ireland in 918 and went to England to assume control over the Viking territories in Northumbria. Consequently, the Vikings could exert their influence over a large portion of the British Isles, ranging from Dublin in the west to York in the east.

Western Viking equipped with axe and shield. (*Photo and copyright by Sjörvaldar Vikings*)

Between 914 and 922, the Vikings created a series of permanent settlements in southern Ireland in order to secure their grip on the island, notably at Waterford, Cork, Wexford and Limerick. Gradually, the Scandinavians living in these settlements started to mix with the local Irish population, initiating a period of co-existence that was based on intermarriage. A new mixed culture emerged, that of the Norse-Gaels, which had a solid presence in southern Ireland and was quite strong from a

Eastern Viking with helmet having nasal and aventail of mail. (*Photo and copyright by Jomsborg Vikings Hird*)

military point of view. However, they were always considered as potentially hostile 'half-foreigners' by the Irish communities in the centre and north of the island. In 919, a large military coalition, comprising most of the Irish kingdoms, sent an army to expel the Vikings of Sitric from their lands. Like in 902, the main target of the Irish was Dublin. A decisive battle was fought at Islandbridge, which resulted in a great Viking victory: hundreds of Irishmen were killed, together with six of their kings. The Battle of Islandbridge broke the Irish military coalition, and the Vikings could continue their expansion across the island.

Ragnall died in 920, Sitric replacing him as the leader of Scandinavian Northumbria. As a result, a new leader named Gofraid emerged among the Vikings of Ireland. After this change of leadership, Gofraid launched a series of offensive campaigns in Ulster, with the objective of conquering the eastern half of Ireland. Between 921 and 927, however, the Vikings were not able to achieve any significant results in Ulster due to strong Irish opposition. The Irish resistance was guided at this time by Muirchertach mac Néill, a capable warlord who had great military skills. In 927, Sitric died and Gofraid went to York to replace him as the leader of Northumbria. Once in England, however, Gofraid was defeated by another pretender to the title and was forced to return to Dublin without having achieved his objective. During his absence, a civil war had erupted among the Vikings of Ireland, with those from Limerick attacking their compatriots in Dublin, which they occupied. After his return Gofraid was able to reconquer Dublin but could not crush the Limerick rebels. The conflict between Dublin and Limerick continued after Gofraid's death in 934, and only ended in 937 when the Vikings of Ireland were again unified under the leadership of Gofraid's heir. In the same year, the Irish Vikings formed a strong military alliance with the Kingdoms of Alba and Strathclyde against the Saxons of England, in an attempt to increase their influence over the British Isles. However, this large anti-Saxon alliance was defeated decisively at the Battle of Brunanburh (which cost the Kingdom of Strathclyde its independence). In 944, during a new age of internal conflicts for the Scandinavians of Ireland, an Irish army was able to attack and sack Dublin, but this was only a short-lived victory as a Viking counter-offensive soon followed.

During the period from 950–980, the Vikings of Ireland formed a series of temporary alliances with various Irish rulers, taking part in several conflicts that ravaged the island to pursue their own interests. By that time, the Scandinavian settlement of Dublin was quite large, being organized as a proper 'kingdom'. In 980, however, the Vikings were defeated at the Battle of Tara by an alliance of Irish rulers who wanted to eliminate the Scandinavian presence in southern Ireland. According to contemporary sources, the Battle of Tara was a massacre for the Vikings, who

Eastern Viking with helmet and kaftan. (*Photo and copyright by Jomsborg Vikings Hird*)

Western Viking equipped with double-handed axe and scramasax dagger. (*Photo and copyright by Sjórvaldar Vikings*)

suffered heavy casualties. After the clash, the Irish forces besieged Dublin and obliged the Vikings to surrender a large number of slaves and valuables in exchange for their lives. The clash at Tara was a turning point in the long history of the Irish Vikings, marking the beginning of their decline. After the battle, the King of Dublin had to submit to the High King of Ireland.

During the closing decades of the tenth century, a prominent new military leader emerged among the Irish aristocrats: Brian Boru, King of Munster since 978 and one of the greatest historical figures of the Irish Middle Ages. In 977, even before becoming ruler of Munster, Brian obtained an important victory over the Vikings of Limerick and annexed their territory to his possessions. One of the key elements of his policy was to expel all the Vikings from the lands of Ireland once and for all. The warlord had a precise political vision: to become 'High King' of Ireland by uniting all its realms against the Vikings in a single national effort. Initially, Brian Boru spent most of his energies in conducting minor wars against the other Irish monarchs, since he needed to impose his will across southern Ireland before opening hostilities with the Vikings. By that time, the Norse-Gaels had lost most of their unity, with each Viking settlement in Ireland pursuing its own interests; there was, for example, a strong rivalry between Limerick and Waterford that was exploited to his advantage by Brian Boru, who concluded a temporary alliance with the Vikings of Waterford before conquering Limerick. The Scandinavians were well integrated into the Irish political system, their settlements acting exactly like the small Irish realms, but their presence was still perceived as a potential threat by most of the Irish population, a factor that Brian Boru intended to use in his favour in order to become the sole ruler of Ireland. Munster and Leinster fought each other from 982 in a series of violent conflicts to determine the ascendancy of one kingdom or the other. From a military point of view, due to the continuous wars fought against the Vikings, Munster and Leinster were the strongest realms in Ireland and their resources were practically equivalent, so the role played by the Norse-Gaels was going to be decisive in determining which kingdom emerged victorious. In 997, after suffering several setbacks, the monarch of Leinster was forced to submit to Brian Boru and recognized his supremacy over southern Ireland.

In 999, Brian had to face a military coalition organized against him which comprised the Kingdoms of Leinster and Dublin. Leinster had not yet fully accepted Munster's dominance over southern Ireland, while the Dublin Vikings were seeking to regain their autonomy by freeing themselves from Irish political influence. The Irishmen of Leinster and the Norse-Gaels of Dublin assembled a large military force, which included a substantial number of Vikings. Brian Boru faced them at the head of an army that deployed warriors from Munster as well as the Kingdom of Meath. At that

Eastern Viking equipped with spear and shield. (*Photo and copyright by Jomsborg Vikings Hird*)

Western Viking with fur cap and axe. (*Photo and copyright by Sjórvaldar Vikings*)

time, the monarchs of Meath held the honorific title of High Kings of Ireland, but their power was gradually declining in favour of Brian Boru's Kingdom of Munster. On 30 December 999, the warriors of Munster and Meath met their enemies from Leinster and Dublin at the Battle of Glenmama. The clash took place in a narrow valley that had been the site of one of Leinster's strongholds for centuries. According to ancient sources, the battle was a massacre, the warriors of both sides fighting with incredible determination; the Vikings of Dublin alone lost around 7,000 men. Glenmama was a triumph for Brian Boru, who captured the ruler of Leinster and continued his advance towards Dublin. Since 980 and until revolting in 999, Dublin had been under the influence of the Kingdom of Meath, but the ascendancy of Brian was to change all that. He entered Dublin without meeting any serious opposition and burned the settlement, plundering and killing with great violence. After these events, the Kingdom of Dublin submitted to Munster and started to provide military contingents to Brian Boru, who then turned against his allies from the Kingdom of Meath with the ambition of becoming the new High King of Ireland. By 1002, after two years of war, the ruler of Meath submitted to Brian, who could finally assume his long-desired honorific title. A single monarch now controlled, directly or indirectly, four of the most important Irish kingdoms: Munster, Leinster, Dublin and Meath.

During the period from 1002–1011, Brian Boru conducted a series of campaigns in northern Ireland, with the objective of submitting the Kingdoms of Uí Néill and Ulaid. The latter had not been greatly affected by the Viking incursions, and had never been dominated by any realm from southern Ireland. By 1011, despite experiencing several difficulties, Brian was able to obtain the submission of every single Irish monarch, and thus was the first king in the history of the island who could exert his political influence over the south as well as the north. In 1012, however, a major revolt broke out against Brian involving Munster's long-time enemies: the Kingdoms of Uí Néill, Leinster and Dublin. They formed a strong military coalition in the hope of breaking Munster's dominance over Ireland. The allied kings knew full well that Brian was much stronger than them from a military point of view, so had no choice but to look for warriors from outside Ireland. Sigtrygg Silkbeard, the King of Dublin, was sent to the Orkney Islands and the Isle of Man to raise large numbers of Viking mercenaries. By promising the crown of Ireland to the Scandinavians, he obtained the support of Sigurd Hlodvirsson (the Earl of Orkney) and Brodir of Man. While Brian Boru camped outside the city of Dublin with his army, several thousand Scandinavian warriors journeyed to Ireland to support his enemies. It must be remembered that at the same time, the Danish Vikings were conquering much of England, so the possibility that Ireland could also become part of the Scandinavian domain was not so remote. The Viking fleets from the Orkney Islands and the Isle of Man reached the port of Dublin during the Easter Holy Week of 1014. With the arrival of the Vikings, the anti-Munster coalition could deploy a total of 7,000 warriors, matching the forces of Brian. The outcome of the upcoming clash would be decided by valour and the skills of the military commanders, rather than by superior numbers. The Battle of Clontarf was fought just north of Dublin between two similarly equipped armies. Brian's enemies deployed in three lines: in the first there were the Scandinavian newcomers, behind which were the Norse-Gaels from the Kingdom of Dublin, with the third line comprising the Irishmen from the Kingdom of Leinster. According to ancient sources, Brian also deployed some allied Irish Vikings among his warriors from Munster. The ensuing clash was extremely violent, since both sides knew they would have little chance of survival if defeated. Brian's son, in particular, fought with enormous courage against his Viking opponents, killing many of them. The Vikings from the Orkney Islands and the Isle of Man were all equipped with chainmail, while the warriors from Munster mostly fought as light skirmishers armed with throwing javelins. Thanks to their superior mobility, the Irishmen were able to cause severe losses to their opponents. The Battle of Clontarf lasted all day, with neither side seeming strong enough to gain the upper hand. Eventually, however, the warriors from Dublin and Leinster broke, which obliged the Scandinavians to also fall back in search of safety. The ensuing retreat of the Vikings turned into a massacre when they were slowed down by crossing the River Tolka during their retreat towards Dublin. When the Vikings finally reached their warships, they learned that the tide had already come in again and all their vessels had been carried away on it. At this point, in a desperate situation, they had no choice but to fight on the beach to the last man. Many Vikings were drowned during this final phase of the clash, but their leaders continued to fight with enormous courage. Murchard, the son and heir of Brian Boru, killed the Earl of Orkney, Sigurd, but shortly afterwards he himself was killed. Brodir of Man killed Brian Boru, but in turn was struck down by Brian's brother, Ulf the Quarrelsome.

While Clontarf was a great victory for Munster, marking the end of the Viking Age in Ireland, it was also the beginning of a great political crisis caused by the sudden death of Brian Boru and his direct heir. The high degree of political unity that had been reached in Ireland under Brian was completely lost, leading to the start of a new season of internecine conflicts. In 1052, the Kingdom of Dublin was annexed by the Kingdom of Leinster, thus bringing to an end the Scandinavian presence in the future Irish capital. After the Irish conquest of Limerick in 977 and of Dublin in 1052, the smaller Viking settlements in Ireland continued to exist for some time, but they were rapidly transformed into minor political entities that were absorbed by the major Irish kingdoms.

Eastern Viking armed with spear. (*Photo and copyright by Jomsborg Vikings Hird*)

Chapter 9

The Kingdom of the Isles

During their incursions against mainland Britain and Ireland, the Vikings frequently operated from naval bases located on minor islands surrounding the British Isles. This was part of their strategy to establish logistic centres not far from their usual targets. Since the Saxons, Picts and Scoti all had limited comparable naval capabilities, the Vikings could easily create an 'empire of the isles' around mainland Britain by conquering all its minor islands. The Vikings divided the islands into two major groups: the 'Northern Islands' and the 'Southern Islands'. The first comprised the Shetlands and the Orkneys, which remained under a strong Norwegian influence for most of the Middle Ages, while the second included the Hebrides, the Isle of Man and the islands of the Firth of Clyde. The Southern Islands were progressively assembled into a Scandinavian realm, known as the 'Kingdom of the Isles', which existed as an independent political entity until the second half of the thirteenth century.

Shetland Islands: The Shetlands, located in the extreme north of the British Isles, were inhabited by sparse communities of Picts before the arrival of the first Viking raiders. Due to their relative proximity to Norway, they soon became the target of frequent Scandinavian incursions. During the late eighth century, while Viking attacks against Britain and Scotland were still sporadic, the Shetlands were rapidly colonized and transformed into a base for their sea-faring raids. They were officially annexed to Norway in 875 and were united with the Orkney Islands to form an earldom that was assigned to the leading Viking warlord, Rognvald Eysteinsson. During the closing decades of the tenth century, the inhabitants of the Shetland Islands converted to Christianity. By this time, the Earls of Orkney, who also ruled over the Shetlands, exerted their control over the Viking footholds in the Highlands (Caithness and Sutherland). From 1196, in order to retain possession of their lands on the Scottish mainland, the Earls of Orkney agreed to become fiefs of the Kingdom of Alba while remaining fiefs of the Kingdom of Norway. Apparently, however, the Shetlands remained under sole Norwegian influence, unlike the Orkneys. During the first half of the thirteenth century, Scottish influence over the Orkneys and Shetlands became increasingly strong; from 1231, for example, the earls who controlled the

Eastern Viking equipped
with double-handed axe
and scramasax dagger.
(*Photo and copyright by
Jomsborg Vikings Hird*)

Western Viking with spear and shield. (*Photo and copyright by Sjórvaldar Vikings*)

islands were all nobles from the Scottish mainland and not from Scandinavia. In 1263, war broke out between the Kingdom of Scotland and the Kingdom of Norway when the Norwegian monarch wanted to expand his possessions from the Orkneys to the Highlands. The conflict did not last long, ending in complete failure for the Norwegians. The ensuing Treaty of Perth, signed in 1266 between Scotland and Norway, confirmed Norwegian suzerainty over the Orkneys and Shetlands. The Shetlands were officially ceded to Scotland by the Kingdom of Norway only in 1471.

Orkney Islands: Before the arrival of the Vikings, the Orkneys were part of the Pictish Kingdom of Fortriu. The first Scandinavian incursions against the islands took place during the late eighth century and were soon followed by an age of progressive colonization. The Orkneys became the main headquarters of the Viking warships operating against Scotland. From 875, the Orkney Islands came under Norwegian control and were united with the Shetlands in order to form an autonomous earldom. After converting to Christianity during the latter part of the tenth century, the inhabitants of the Orkneys gradually came under the joint influence of Norway and Scotland since their earls had some possessions in the Highlands. From 1231, both the Orkneys and the Shetlands started to be ruled by aristocrats from mainland Scotland rather than Norway. In 1471, the Orkney Islands were annexed to the Kingdom of Scotland, as were the Shetland Islands.

Hebrides Islands: Prior to the early Scandinavian incursions, the Inner Hebrides were part of the Kingdom of Dál Riata, while the Outer Hebrides were part of the Kingdom of Fortriu. Consequently, the former were inhabited by the Scoti and the latter by Picts. Due to their strategic position, the Hebrides were raided several times during the early decades of the ninth century and soon became an important base for the Vikings. They came under direct Norwegian control around 885, but this did not last for long, since they revolted against Harald Fairhair of Norway to regain their autonomy. The Norwegian warlord sent one of his best men, Ketill Flatnose, to the Hebrides with orders to crush the rebellion, but Ketill occupied the islands for himself and started to rule them as an independent monarch. This marked the birth of the Kingdom of the Isles, a Viking realm centred on the Hebrides. In 990, Sigurd the Stout, Earl of Orkney, took control of the Hebrides, but this political change did not last for long as the Kingdom of the Isles regained its independence in 1014. During the following years, the Vikings of Dublin started to exert a solid influence over the Hebrides as well as the Isle of Man (which came under direct control of the Kingdom of Dublin for some time). In 1079, the Isle of Man also became part of the Kingdom of the Isles, after having been an autonomous Scandinavian possession for several decades. Some years later, in 1098, the Norwegians sent a fleet to retake control of the Kingdom of the Isles. However, this attempt failed, so the Hebrides continued to be ruled as an autonomous Scandinavian realm. The twelfth century was characterized by a series of internal conflicts for the Kingdom of the Isles, which were complicated by the external influences exerted by Norway and Scotland. These 'civil wars' saw the temporary separation of the Inner Hebrides from the Kingdom of the Isles and a series of naval battles. Nevertheless, the Kingdom of the Isles survived as an independent state after this turbulent era, albeit definitively losing its original 'piratical' nature. From 1164, the reunified realm started to be ruled by Norse-Gael nobles from Scotland, who became known as 'Lords of the Isles' and had strong links with the Scottish mainland. These aristocrats were fiefs of Norway as 'Kings of the Isles', but also fiefs of Scotland since they had some rich possessions on the Scottish mainland. In 1249 a large Scottish fleet, commanded by King Alexander II, tried to occupy the Kingdom of the Isles but failed completely; this event led to the Norwegian expedition of 1263 against Scotland and finally to the signing of the Treaty of Perth in 1266. This treaty gave the Hebrides and the Isle of Man to the Kingdom of Scotland, and thus put an end to the long history of the Kingdom of the Isles.

Eastern Viking with double-handed axe and helmet having nasal. (*Photo and copyright by Jomsborg Vikings Hird*)

Eastern Viking with fur cap and axe. Note the long scramasax dagger carried on the waist. (*Photo and copyright by Confraternita del Leone/Historia Viva*)

Isle of Man: Being located between Ireland and Scotland, and between the Viking centres of Dublin and York, the Isle of Man always had a great strategic importance for the Vikings. During the period from 800–815, the island was plundered several times by Scandinavian raiders, who were initially interested only in plunder and capturing slaves. By 880, however, the first permanent Scandinavian settlements had been established on the Isle of Man. Between 990 and 1079, the island came under the direct rule of the Kingdom of Dublin, which was attracted by the naval potential of the island. In 1079, the Isle of Man was absorbed into the Kingdom of the Isles. When the latter ceased to be an independent realm, the Isle of Man became part of the Kingdom of Scotland according to the Treaty of Perth (1266).

Firth of Clyde: The mouth of the River Clyde and its nearby islands were the heart of the Kingdom of Dál Riata before the arrival of the Vikings. The early Scandinavian raids in the region were destructive and lasted for several decades, until the dawn of a new age of permanent settlement by the Vikings. Despite being quite small and having a tiny population, the islands of the Clyde became an important Viking naval base and were absorbed into the Kingdom of the Isles. For some periods, the Vikings settled on the small islands also exerted their control over the mouth of the River Clyde. The Firth of Clyde marked the boundary between the Kingdom of Scotland and the Kingdom of the Isles until the latter disappeared from history in 1266.

Chapter 10

The Vikings in France and the Siege of Paris

France, together with England, was one of the main targets of Scandinavian raids during the two centuries of the Viking Age. Normandy, in particular, was greatly exposed to Viking attacks due to its geographical position; being a peninsula stretching from northern France towards southern England, it was a perfect location for Viking naval bases. Normandy's name derives from 'Northmannia', a term that can be translated as 'Land of the Norsemen'. When Scandinavian incursions in France began, France was still part of the mighty Carolingian Empire that had been created by the Frankish king, Charlemagne. At the height of its power, the Frankish Empire dominated most of continental Europe: from Catalonia in northern Spain to the lands of the Frisians in the Netherlands, from Brittany in north-western France to the heart of Germany. When Charlemagne, one of the Middle Ages' greatest military leaders, died in early 814, he had transformed Europe during his long reign, uniting most of the Germanic kingdoms that had emerged from the collapse of the Roman Empire into a single political entity. The great monarch was succeeded by his son, Louis the Pious, who was able to preserve the unity of the Carolingian Empire despite the emergence of the Vikings and the outbreak of some bloody civil wars inside Frankish lands. When Louis the Pious died in 840, a civil war broke out between his three sons, each of whom wanted to become emperor and had no intention of renouncing his claims. The internecine hostilities finally came to an end only in the summer of 843, when the Treaty of Verdun was signed between the three pretenders to the Carolingian throne. According to its terms, the vast Frankish Empire was divided into three new states: West Francia, Middle Francia and East Francia. West Francia, roughly corresponding to present-day France, was given to Charles the Bald. Middle Francia, comprising the Rhineland and northern Italy, was assigned to Lothair I, who also inherited the imperial title. East Francia, composed of most of western Germany, became the domain of Louis the German. The three new states had different destinies. West Francia gradually became the Kingdom of France, while East Francia later became the Holy Roman Empire. The lands of Middle Francia, however, ceased to be autonomous in 870 when the Treaty of Meerssen partitioned them between Charles the Bald and Louis the German.

Eastern Viking with Gjermundbu Helmet and padded armour. (*Photo and copyright by Jomsborg Vikings Hird*)

Western Viking with helmet having nasal. (*Photo and copyright by Brokkar Lag*)

Due to the frequent civil wars and many territorial changes during the period from 840–870, the territories of the former Carolingian Empire became extremely weak from a military point of view. This was of great help to the Vikings, who could attack the individual Frankish communities without having to face large armies. As mentioned above, most of the Scandinavian raids conducted on mainland Europe had as their target the emerging Kingdom of France, or West Francia. Some early Viking incursions in France took place during the very last years of Charlemagne's reign, but it was under Charles the Bald that they became a significant problem for the French monarchy. The first recorded Scandinavian attack in France took place during 799, and was soon followed by several others. In response to these early raids, around 810, Charlemagne organized a form of coastal defence in the northern regions of his empire, but this measure was never fully implemented. In 820, during the reign of his son Louis the Pious, a major Scandinavian incursion was repulsed at the mouth of the River Seine. The Vikings launched a new attack against Frisia, on the territory of present-day Netherlands, in 834, achieving some success. The following years saw an escalation of raids: Antwerp, Rouen and Nantes were all attacked by the Vikings, who were exploiting the weakness of the Frankish military system (heavily involved in the ongoing internecine conflicts).

In March 845, a large fleet of Danish Vikings, with 120 warships, entered the Seine under command of Ragnar Lodbrok. The target of the raiders was Paris, one of the richest cities of West Francia (capital of the kingdom since 987). Charles the Bald was determined to fight to the death in order to defend the city, and thus soon mobilized his military forces, dividing them in two parts: one was deployed on the eastern bank of the Seine, the other on the western bank. At that time, Paris was still relatively small, not extending beyond the Ile de la Cité, a natural river island located in the middle of the Seine. After defeating one of the two Frankish armies and killing all the captured men in order to spread terror, Ragnar and his raiders landed on the Ile de la Cité on Easter Sunday. The Scandinavians plundered Paris with great violence, killing many civilians. After several days, having obtained everything they wanted, they decided to leave the French city, partly because a plague had broken out inside their camp (at the time, the banks of the Seine were covered by marshes and were characterized by a quite inhospitable environment). Before returning home, however, the Vikings obliged Charles the Bald to pay them an immense sum of money: 7,000 French pounds of gold and silver. This was just the first danegeld paid by the Frankish monarchs to the Vikings, which was followed by several others. In the 840s, the Scandinavians attacked and pillaged several locations in Normandy, such as Rouen, with a predilection for the richest religious sites. Thanks to the presence of many navigable rivers, the Vikings could easily move across northern and central

France. The Franks were surprised by the Vikings' ability to sail up-river, and thus could do little to counter the enemy attacks. By penetrating deeply into the heart of France, the Vikings understood that the country could easily be conquered by them.

As time progressed, the Vikings started to attack the interior lands of the Western Franks with more frequency and larger numbers of warships. The Frankish military system, based on elite field armies that were too large to be moved rapidly, lacked the flexibility to create highly mobile task forces that could resist the Scandinavian raids taking place along the rivers. In 864, Charles the Bald tried to resolve this problem by issuing the so-called 'Edict of Pistres', which contained a series of practical measures aimed at protecting French cities and rural areas from the attacks of the Vikings. With the new edict, the Frankish monarch created a large force of cavalry that had to serve on a permanent basis as a special anti-raider corps. All French subjects who were able-bodied and owned a horse had to enlist in the new cavalry force, and could be called to serve with very short notice by the royal authorities. The high mobility of cavalry would counter the rapidity of the Scandinavian raids and enable the French to attack the invaders before they could re-embark on their warships and sail away from France. The Edict of Pistres also contained other important measures, such as an to build fortified bridges at all the towns located on navigable rivers. These would preven the Vikings from sailing into the interior of France or transporting large amounts of booty on their ships after completing their incursions. Unluckily for the French, however, few of the various local communities had the resources to build new fortified bridges, and thus only a few of them were constructed. The edict promulgated by Charles the Bald further prohibited all trade in weapons with the Scandinavians, while selling horses to the Vikings was also forbidden and any infraction to the new measures was punishable by death. Charles the Bald's main objective was to prevent the Vikings from establishing permanent bases in his realm. Following the Edict of Pistres, many French nobles started to build castles and fortifications on their territories in order to defend their peasant communities from the constant threat of Viking invasion. Yet the building of private castles did nothing but reduce the power of central government and the control that it had over the many nobles of the Kingdom of France (who became increasingly autonomous, ruling as local monarchs).

During their incursions against Normandy, the Vikings understood that the nearby region of Brittany resented Frankish rule and thus were able to conclude an important military alliance with the Bretons. The latter were of Celtic descent and had only been subjugated by the Franks during the reign of Charlemagne. They had strong cultural links with the Britons of Wales and had always tried to preserve their 'national' autonomy as much as possible. To counter the Viking colonization

Eastern Viking with sword and shield. (*Photo and copyright by Jomsborg Vikings Hird*)

Western Viking equipped with heavy spear and chainmail. (*Photo and copyright by Jomsborg Vikings Hird*)

of Normandy and block the initiatives of the Scandinavian/Breton alliance, Charles the Bald created the new 'march' (military region) of Neustria on the eastern borders of Normandy. This was garrisoned by significant military forces and was under the control of Robert the Strong, who was one of the most experienced Frankish warlords. In 866, a joint Viking/Breton force launched a massive incursion into the territory of Neustria, raiding areas such as Anjou and Maine. Robert of Neustria responded by mobilizing his troops and asking for the help of other leading French nobles, most notably Rainulf I, Duke of Aquitaine. The Frankish forces, mostly consisting of cavalry, succeeded in intercepting the Viking/Breton raiders before they could re-embark on their warships and returning to their bases by sailing along the River Loire. A pitched battle soon followed, with the Frankish forces defeated and suffering severe losses, while both Robert of Neustria and Rainulf of Aquitaine were killed. The following year, after such a severe defeat, Charles the Bald had no choice but to come to terms with his enemies. He recognized the leader of the Bretons as King of Brittany and ceded the Cotentin Peninsula to them. Despite this, the Vikings continued to ravage the valley of the Loire during the following years, sacking Bourges, Orléans and Angers. After their previous success, the Vikings launched another three minor incursions against Paris during the 860s. In response to these attacks, Charles the Bald promulgated the Edict of Pistres that has been analyzed above. The edict was applied with a degree of efficiency in the Ile de la Cité, where two new fortified bridges were built across the Seine to stop the Viking longships (one on each side of the island). Paris was heavily fortified during the 870s to combat future Scandinavian attacks. Meanwhile, the Viking raids continued on a large scale. During 880 and 881, the Scandinavian warriors suffered minor setbacks at the Battle of Thimeon (north of the River Sambre) and the Battle of Saucourt-en-Vimeu (near Abbeville). These reverses, however, did not change the general situation in favour of the Franks, who were still in the process of reorganizing their military forces.

In 885, the Vikings launched their largest attack against France, which resulted in the famous Siege of Paris. Three hundred warships with 12,000 warriors entered the mouth of the Seine, with the objective of creating a permanent settlement in northern France. Odo, Count of Paris, was well prepared to meet the invaders: the two new low-lying footbridges of his city (one made of wood and the other of stone) would block the passage of the Viking ships. Before their arrival, he built a tower at the head of each bridge to strengthen his defences against attacks from the banks of the Seine. After reaching Paris, the Vikings demanded the payment of a large sum of money, but Odo refused to come to terms and siege operations began. The Scandinavians first attacked the north-eastern tower, which protected the wooden bridge. They were repulsed with heavy losses by the French defenders, who employed a deadly mixture of hot wax and pitch to stop the assault. During the following days, the Vikings bombarded the city with siege engines and tried to destroy the bridge with fire, but all their attempts failed due to the sturdy resistance of the defenders. The Vikings maintained the siege for two months, building trenches and raiding the nearby countryside in search of supplies. In January 886, they tried to fill the river shallows with debris and vegetation in order to get around the besieged tower, but they eventually decided to change strategy and send three burning warships against the wooden bridge in a bid to destroy it. The impact of the burning warships caused serious damage to the bridge, which collapsed a few days later when rain caused the debris-filled river to overflow. The tower's remaining twelve defenders refused to surrender and were all killed by the Vikings. The attackers then divided their forces in two: one remained on the eastern bank of the Seine in front of Paris, while the other sailed up-river to pillage as much as possible. Le Mans, Chartres and Evreux were all attacked by the raiders, who entered the course of the River Loire in order to sack more urban centres. In May 886, disease began to spread among the ranks of Paris' defenders. With the situation becoming desperate for the Franks, Odo was left with no choice but to abandon the city in search of reinforcements. He was later able to return to Paris at the head of a French royal army and to enter the city over the stone bridge. By that time, a large part of the besieging forces had already decided to return home, and the leadership of the Vikings who had remained around Paris was now in the hands of a warlord named Rollo. After another failed attack against the Ile de la Cité and the arrival of substantial Frankish reinforcements, Rollo finally accepted a payment of 700 pounds of silver in exchange for leaving Paris. Odo, whose efforts had saved the city, became King of France in 888.

Although Paris was now safe, the Vikings' raids in France continued during the following decades. They were mostly directed against Normandy, where the Scandinavians were finally able to create some permanent settlements around their naval bases, under the guidance of Rollo. In 911, in an attempt to regularize the Viking presence inside the boundaries of his realm, the new King of France, Charles the Simple, decided to sign a treaty with them. According to its terms, Rollo was given substantial portions of Norman territory for his men in exchange for his formal submission to the Kingdom of France. The Vikings had to promise that they would defend the territory of Normandy from the attacks of other Scandinavian groups, and also had to convert to Christianity. In essence, Rollo had agreed to become a vassal of Charles the Simple in exchange for possession of a vast territory in northern France. In 933, the Vikings of Normandy extended their domains by annexing the Cotentin Peninsula of Brittany, which had been colonized by groups of Norwegian Vikings.

Western Viking with hood and chainmail. (*Photo and copyright by Jomsborg Vikings Hird*)

Eastern Viking with Gjermundbu
Helmet and heavy spear. (*Photo and
copyright by Brokkar Lag*)

Western Viking with helmet having nasal and aventail of mail. (*Photo and copyright by Jomsborg Vikings Hird*)

Western Viking equipped with helmet and chainmail. (*Photo and copyright by Jomsborg Vikings Hird*)

Within a few generations, the Scandinavians living in Normandy had intermarried with the natives and adopted many aspects of their culture. As a result, around 990, the Viking territories of northern France were officially organized as the Duchy of Normandy and started to develop a proper feudal organization.

While these events took place in northern France, where some form of centralized state existed since the signing of the Treaty of Verdun, the Vikings also pillaged many settlements in southern France, where the Duchy of Aquitaine was ravaged by internal conflicts. Employed by the local aristocrats as mercenaries, the Vikings were able to establish a base at the mouth of the River Garonne, from which they launched many incursions against the very heart of France.

Between 810 and 884, the Scandinavians also attacked the coastline of present-day Belgium and the Netherlands several times, plundering many settlements and establishing a number of permanent bases. Politically, these regions were formally part of West Francia, but in practice they were abandoned to their destiny since the Franks did not have a fleet that could defend them from Viking incursions. Frisia, the northern portion of the Netherlands, was particularly exposed since it bordered the southern part of Denmark and thus could also be attacked by the Vikings on land. The Frisians, however, were one of the few Germanic communities of the Frankish Empire who did know how to build effective warships, and had good sea-faring capabilities. Consequently, they organized a strong resistance against the raiders. An extensive system of dikes and seawalls was built in order to protect the coastline from Scandinavian landings. Despite all their efforts, however, the Frisians could not prevent the Vikings from establishing several bases on their territory. In 850, Lothair I, the Carolingian emperor, had no choice but to acknowledge the Scandinavian warlord Rorik of Dorestad as his vassal and the ruler of a large portion of Frisia. During 879, a large Viking force commanded by the Danish leader Godfrid established a base at Ghent and rapidly assumed control over the whole of Frisia. In 884, at the Battle of Norditi, the Frisians decisively defeated the Viking invaders, who were surprised by the incoming tide during the retreat that followed the clash and suffered heavy losses. After this encounter, the Vikings ceased to be a menace for the Frisians, who started to have a higher degree of political autonomy inside the Holy Roman Empire.

Chapter 11

The Viking Colonization of the Northern Atlantic

T he Vikings are well known as pirates and conquerors, but they were also the most important explorers of the Middle Ages. Indeed, thanks to their great sea-faring capabilities, they were able to navigate across the northern part of the Atlantic Ocean and reach the coastline of North America after having colonized several lands: the Faroe Islands, Iceland and Greenland. The explorative successes of the Scandinavians were mostly due to the great quality of their longships, but also to their courage. Before them, no one had ever attempted to sail across the Atlantic in search of new lands. The Vikings believed that the world had precise limits, and thus, when navigating westwards, they believed they were moving towards the boundaries of the known world. Their journey was an extremely risky one, because the Atlantic Ocean was much larger and more dangerous than they could have expected. Despite this, by moving from one island to the next, the Vikings were able to travel beyond the limits of medieval knowledge to find a new land of opportunities where their expanding communities could flourish. The real protagonists of the Scandinavian explorations across the Atlantic were the Norwegian Vikings, who were used to navigating far from their coastline and who had some excellent naval bases in the fjords of their homeland. These bases were perfect for protecting anchored ships and building new vessels in total safety. The expeditions departing from the fjords were destined to discover new lands that were located very far from Europe. Moving from Norway, during the early decades of the ninth century, the Vikings reached the Faroe Islands, north of the Shetlands, a key position for any navigator interested in exploring the Atlantic. According to the latest research, the Faroe Islands were already inhabited before the arrival of the first Scandinavians. These early communities, probably coming from Scotland, were too small to be significant and thus were easily colonized by the Vikings. According to Viking tradition, the first Scandinavian to reach the Faroe Islands was a man named Grimur Kamban. It is probable, however, that he was the first to settle on the islands, not the first to discover them, since the Vikings had sailed across that area of the Atlantic for many years. Over the years, the Scandinavian communities living on the Faroe Islands started to flourish, thanks to crop cultivation and the raising of livestock. The Vikings on the Faroe Islands were peaceful farmers rather than warriors. They did not use their islands as bases for

Eastern Viking warlord with full
personal equipment. (*Photo and
copyright by Brokkar Lag*)

Western Viking with axe and shield. (*Photo and copyright by Jomsborg Vikings Hird*)

launching piratical raids, and adopted a quite democratic form of government: all free men of the islands were part of a council, which made laws and solved disputes. Around the year 1000, the inhabitants of the Faroe Islands converted to Christianity and a few years later, in 1035, their territory officially became part of Norway. Apparently, both the conversion and the annexation to Norway were the result of an internecine conflict that saw the inhabitants of the northern Faroe Islands attacking those of the southern isles. The history of the Faroe Islands remained linked to that of Norway for the next four centuries, seeing no major political changes.

Between the Faroe Islands and Iceland is a distance of 450 miles, which was a vast one for the standards of early Middle Ages maritime navigation. It seems that Iceland had already been visited by several navigators before the arrival of the Vikings. According to recent studies, some semi-permanent outposts were built on Iceland's coastline between 770 and 870. These were inhabited only during the summer months and were probably used for fishing. Whatever the case, before the arrival of the Vikings, the few navigators from Scotland who had built these outposts had not been able to establish a permanent presence on Iceland. After having explored the coastline of the island for several years and determined that Iceland could be settled, the first Vikings landed around 874. Within a few decades they were able to cover most of the island with new rural settlements, which soon started to flourish. The first expedition probably consisted of just 300–400 individuals, but these were soon followed by more than 20,000 settlers during the subsequent decades. By the time of the Scandinavians' arrival, the climate of Iceland was relatively warm, which allowed them to practise agriculture profitably. As a result, the colonization of the island was the perfect answer to the problems of over-population that were being experienced by Norway. In addition, unlike the British Isles, Iceland could be easily settled by the Vikings since there were no native communities to defend their homeland from the arrival of the newcomers. By 930, the Scandinavians had completed their settlement of the island, which was now covered with 1,500 farms that were inhabited by 24,000 individuals. Similarly to what happened in the Faroe Islands, the Vikings of Iceland adopted a quite democratic constitution and established an assembly – named the Alþingi – that was attended by all the free men. The Icelandic Vikings were peaceful individuals and capable farmers, whose communities flourished thanks to naval trade.

The Scandinavian communities in Iceland continued to live in peace and prosperity until 1220, when the so-called 'Age of the Sturlungs' began. This was characterized by two main elements: the attempts to seize control of the island by the Kingdom of Norway and the internecine conflicts fought between the most prominent Icelandic families. It was during the Age of the Sturlungs, in 1238, that the largest battle in the history of Iceland was fought. The population of the island had expanded massively

Eastern Viking warlord with pointed helmet and chainmail. (*Photo and copyright by Brokkar Lag*)

Eastern Viking with Gjermundbu Helmet having aventail of mail. (*Photo and copyright by Jomsborg Vikings Hird*)

during the previous decades, to the point that the warring clans were able to mobilize a total of 2,700 warriors. The Age of the Sturlungs had a very negative impact on the history of Iceland, since the wars between opposing clans significantly reduced the economic capabilities of the island. The Kingdom of Norway took advantage of this situation, annexing Iceland in 1264. This political operation was carried on by the Norwegian monarch Haakon IV, who dreamed of creating a large Norwegian Empire across the Atlantic by uniting the various settlements that had been established by the Vikings during the previous centuries. It was Haakon, for example, who planned the Norwegian expedition against Scotland that has been described in the previous chapters, and who formed a military alliance with the Kingdom of the Isles. A new phase in the history of Iceland began in 1264, and thus the 'Viking Period' came to an end.

Moving from Iceland, the Vikings continued their exploration/settlement of the Atlantic coastlines by reaching Greenland. As is made clear by its name, Greenland was not an inhospitable land during the Middle Ages, being covered with grassland along the southern coast and thus having much cultivable land. Before the arrival of the Scandinavians, Greenland was populated by some sparse communities of Paleo-Eskimo immigrants who came to the island from North America. These Eskimos experienced serious problems in settling Greenland in a permanent way, but were always able to retain a presence on the island. The Vikings became aware of Greenland's existence around 970, when a Scandinavian navigator who was journeying from Norway to Iceland was blown off course by a storm and sighted the coastline of the island. After the seaman finally reached Iceland, the local Vikings were informed of Greenland's existence and the first explorative expeditions then started to be organized. The Scandinavian colonization of Greenland was guided by the most famous of the Viking explorers: Erik the Red. He arrived in Iceland with his family around 950, and was the son of a man who had been banished from Norway. He lived as a farmer on the island for several years, until he was involved into a bloody feud that finally caused his expulsion (for three years) from Iceland. According to Viking sources, Erik was banished from his new homeland around 982, after which he felt he had no option but to organize an expedition to find a new land where he could live. A few years previously, another Viking from Iceland had already journeyed to Greenland to establish the first permanent Viking settlement, but his attempt had failed completely. Erik, being courageous but also desperate, sailed towards the island with the hope of better luck. His expedition rounded the southern tip of Greenland and sailed up the western coast, where he landed. He then conducted inland explorations for three years. After his three years of exile had expired, Erik returned to Iceland, taking with him some very interesting stories about

Eastern Viking equipped with lamellar armour. (*Photo and copyright by Brokkar Lag*)

Eastern Viking with
fur cap and chainmail.
(*Photo and copyright by
Jomsborg Vikings Hird*)

the new land that he had explored. Many Icelandic Vikings, especially those living on the poorest lands of the island, were impressed by Erik's tales and decided to join him in an expedition aimed at colonizing Greenland.

Erik the Red returned to Greenland in 985 with a large number of settlers under his orders. However, of the twenty-five ships that left Iceland, only fourteen reached their destination. Sailing in the cold waters of the Northern Atlantic was an extremely difficult undertaking in those times, especially because the Scandinavians did not have full knowledge of Greenland's coastline. Despite the great initial difficulties, Erik's men built two colonies in their new homeland, known as the Eastern Settlement (present-day Qaqortoq) and the Western Settlement (Nuuk). Erik had planned to build more Viking colonies in the interior of the island, but the settlers eventually realized that the sites of their two original settlements were the only areas of Greenland where farms could be established due to the relative fertility of the terrain. The interior of the island was covered with snow and ice for most of the year. The early years of the Scandinavian presence in Greenland were very difficult ones, with the only way for there to be enough food involving hunting in the interior of the island. Every summer, when the weather was more favourable for travel, both the Eastern Settlement and the Western Settlement sent their best men to hunt in Disko Bay, which was above the Arctic Circle. The two groups of hunters collected large amounts of food as well as other valuable commodities such as seals (used to produce ropes) or ivory obtained from walrus tusks. Erik the Red established himself in the Eastern Settlement, where he built a large estate and he assumed the title of 'Paramount Chieftain of Greenland'. Having started his career as a poor exile who had been forced to leave his homeland, he was now greatly respected and very wealthy. The economy of the Eastern Settlement was based on livestock farming and seal hunting. Its population underwent a rapid expansion, and thus, by 1000, there were around 5,000 Viking inhabitants on Greenland. In those years, Iceland was experiencing problems with over-population, so significant numbers of immigrants left their settlements on the island in order to move on to Greenland. In 1002, however, a group of immigrants from Iceland brought with them a deadly epidemic that ravaged Greenland. This killed many of the local inhabitants, including Erik the Red, and marked the beginning of the Eastern Settlement's decline. The settlement became part of the Kingdom of Norway in 1261, after its population had already converted to Christianity (in 1126). The Viking presence in Greenland survived until the early fifteenth century, but gradually became marginal due to climate change (with the temperature of the island becoming colder) and the outbreak of conflicts with the Inuit communities.

The Vikings started to explore the lands located west of Greenland soon after Erik the Red arrived with the first colonists, and thus, at some point, discovered the coastline

Eastern Viking with lamellar armour and loose trousers. (*Photo and copyright by Jomsborg Vikings Hird*)

Eastern Viking with
fur cap and lamellar
armour. (*Photo and
copyright by Jomsborg
Vikings Hird*)

of present-day Canada. According to contemporary sources, a Scandinavian merchant, who was sailing between Iceland and Greenland, was the first to see the coast of North America after having been blown off course by a storm during his voyage. The merchant reported his discovery to Erik the Red's son and successor, Leif Erikson, who quickly organized an expedition to set off from Greenland for the unexplored land that had just been found. Initially, Erik the Red was to have participated in the expedition, but he decided to remain in Greenland while his son assumed command. Leif had a single ship and just forty men under his orders, but despite this he was able to reach North America and land on what became known as Baffin Island. After venturing further by sea, he landed on a forested tract of coastline that he called 'Markland', which corresponds to the present-day Cape Porcupine in Labrador. The Viking explorers were impressed by the natural resources of the lands that they were seeing for the first time: these were covered with woods and crossed by long rivers that were home to thousands of salmon. North America appeared to be the perfect homeland for a Viking, since the abundance of trees was perfect to build ships and the presence of food reserves permitted the creation of stable settlements. As winter approached, Leif decided to encamp on the coastline and to send out small parties to survey the surrounding areas. During their explorations, the Vikings discovered that the region was full of vines and grapes: as a result, they called it 'Vinland'. This area was probably the actual coastline of Labrador. Leif and his men built a semi-permanent settlement and left North America with the coming of spring, returning home with a cargo full of grapes and timber. When Leif reached Greenland in the early months of 1002, it appears that he started planning a new expedition to establish a permanent settlement in North America, but his father's sudden death and the problems then experienced by his home community prevented him from returning to Vinland. Instead, it was Leif's brother, Thorvald, who went to North America in 1004. He found the camp that had been built two years before still intact, and spent the winter months in Vinland. Thorvald was the first Viking to come into contact with the natives of Newfoundland, whom from the outset he considered to be enemies. He attacked a group of natives without reason, killing nine of them. Apparently, the Vikings had no idea of the actual number of the native communities. Indeed, a few days after these events, a large number of native warriors attacked the Viking camp and Thorvald was killed by an enemy arrow. Despite the death of their leader, the Scandinavian explorers remained in Vinland for another year before going back to Greenland.

In 1009, a new Viking expedition went to North America. This time it was commanded by Thorfinn Karlsefni and consisted of three ships that transported 160 colonists, together with livestock. The previous expeditions, organized by Erik the Red's sons, had been too small to permit the establishment of a permanent settlement,

Eastern Viking with fur cap and kaftan. (*Photo and copyright by Brokkar Lag*)

but now, Thorfinn was determined to create a lasting colony on Newfoundland. Differently from his predecessor, he tried to establish a positive relationship with the natives: his colonists, for example, exchanged milk and red cloth for fur and skins provided by the natives. At some point, however, the apparently peaceful situation changed: the natives probably understood that the Vikings were intending to stay

Eastern Viking equipped with Gjermundbu Helmet and lamellar armour. (*Photo and copyright by Jomsborg Vikings Hird*)

and thus decided to attack their settlements with a large number of warriors. The ensuing fighting was particularly violent, since Thorfinn's men were determined to defend their new homeland. Despite all their efforts, however, the Scandinavians were defeated and were forced to abandon the new camps that they had established on Newfoundland. They then remained in their original camp for some time, but in the end they decided to leave North America and go back to Greenland. The natives of Vinland and Greenland were called 'Skraeling' by the Vikings and were extremely warlike, according to Scandinavian sources. We know very little about them, other than that they were surely quite numerous. Their resistance was the main factor behind the failure of the Vikings' colonization of Vineland, since Thorfinn understood that any future settlement in North America would have been under constant threat of attack from the natives. Considering all the various elements, a permanent colonization of North America by the Vikings was impossible from a practical point of view: Vinland was too far from Norway or Iceland, and thus any expedition aimed at exploring North America had to be organized in Greenland. However, the Scandinavian settlements on Greenland were too small and sparsely populated to provide a sufficient number of colonists. Furthermore, there was no central authority governing the exploration of the new lands, so there were problems related to leadership. Initially, the Vikings had hoped that Vinland could be settled without encountering opposition, as had been the case in Iceland and Greenland. In North America, however, they learned that the lands to the west were densely inhabited by a population of warlike natives. We can only imagine what could have happened if the Scandinavian presence in Newfoundland had become a permanent one: America would have been colonized by the Europeans five centuries before it actually was, and the Vikings would have played a prominent role in this historical process. New products would have reached the European markets, while the natives of North America would have been forced to face a new enemy whose military technology was comparable to their own.

With the progressive decline of Greenland, the 'Atlantic empire' established by the Vikings came to an end, leaving behind only a few tangible elements. These were particularly significant in Iceland, since the island immediately became part of the Scandinavian world. The short-lived history of Vinland, however, was forgotten for many centuries, until archaeological finds confirmed the existence of a Viking presence in Canada.

Chapter 12

The Varangians and Kievan Rus'

As we have seen in the previous chapters, the Vikings from Denmark and Norway expanded in Western Europe and across the Atlantic. As for those based in Sweden, they conducted their raids and explorations towards Eastern Europe, and most notably Russia. As has been mentioned above, the Swedish Vikings who settled in Eastern Europe were known as Varangians and proved to be very successful conquerors, just like the Western Vikings who terrorized the British Isles and France for two centuries. Before the appearance of the Scandinavians, Russia was mostly inhabited by the various tribes of the Eastern Slavs, who had settled in a very large area that ranged from the Baltic Sea in the north to the Black Sea in the south. The northern portion of this vast region was covered with dense woods, while the southern part consisted of vast plains that were part of the immense Eurasian steppes. The whole territory of Russia was crossed by long and navigable rivers such as the Volga and the Don, which were to become fundamental waterways for the Vikings. The presence of these rivers enabled the Scandinavians to travel long distances in complete safety and to cross a land of which they knew very little (at least initially). Russia was full of natural resources and had great economic potential due to its strategic position, the lands of the Eastern Slavs being located between the Scandinavian world in the north and the Byzantine Empire in the south. The Varangians soon understood that Russia was a land of great opportunities, as they could create a commercial network that, by using the major rivers of the region, could import massive amounts of goods produced in Scandinavia into the territories of the Byzantine Empire. The Byzantine Empire was the richest and most sophisticated state of medieval Europe, where a distinct civilization had developed after the fall of the Roman Empire in the West. The Varangians soon understood that the Slavs were quite weak militarily, since they were fragmented into many tribes and were not particularly warlike. As a result, the Scandinavian penetration in Russia was quite easy and rapid. South of the Slavs, in the territory of present-day Ukraine, there were the communities of Khazars. These were a nomadic people of the steppes of Turkic stock, and fought mostly as mounted archers equipped with powerful composite bows. Consequently, they were much more warlike than the Slavs and put up a strong resistance against the Varangians.

Eastern Viking with lamellar corselet. (*Photo and copyright by Jomsborg Vikings Hird*)

Western Viking with spear and shield. (*Photo and copyright by Brokkar Lag*)

The Viking expansion in Russia began around 850, in the area of the eastern Baltic that is located south of Finland. Here, the Slavs lived together with some Finnic communities, which controlled most of southern Finland. By 859, the Varangians from Sweden had already been able to impose their rule over the Slav and Finnic tribes living near the Baltic, and received a tribute from them. There was an anti-Varangian revolt in 862, but this did not have long-lasting effects because the internal divisions existing between the Slav and Finnic communities prevented the formation of a solid anti-Scandinavian alliance. Shortly after the end of the revolt, the Slavs decided to 'invite' the Varangians to come to their lands and become their overlords, with the hope that they could keep order and prevent the outbreak of further internecine conflicts. Three powerful Varangian brothers – Rurik, Sineus and Truvor – the leaders of the future Rus' or 'Russi', accepted the invitation and went to Russia at the head of their retainers. They established themselves in Novgorod, not far from the Baltic Sea and on the River Volchov, where they rapidly built an important commercial centre that was connected with all the major waterways of the region. After the death of his two brothers, Rurik became the sole ruler of the Varangians and established the so-called 'Rurik Dynasty', which would dominate the political life of Russia during the following centuries. After the Varangians had secured their position in Novgorod, Rurik sent two of his best men to the southern regions of Russia in order to conduct a long-range exploration. His objective was to reach Constantinople and open a new commercial route with the Byzantine Empire. Askold and Dir, the two warriors chosen to explore southern Russia, were very successful in their mission. On their way south, while crossing the lands of the Khazars in Ukraine, they discovered a small but well-fortified settlement located on a hill and decided to capture it. This would later become the city of Kiev, the most important urban centre of the Varangians in southern Russia. During the following decades, by travelling on the River Dniepr, thousands of Varangians moved from Novgorod to Kiev, which became increasingly important as a commercial centre. The immense lands located between the two Varangian centres were progressively settled by the Scandinavians, who had no problems in overcoming the weak resistance of the local Slavs. The culture of the Varangians and that of the Slavs soon started to meld, creating the basis for the emergence of medieval Russia.

The rise of the Varangians was soon perceived as a menace by the Byzantines, who wanted to retain their political supremacy over the southern region of the Balkans. The Varangians had been impressed by the tales of the foreign navigators who had visited Constantinople: they described the Byzantine capital as a city full of treasures, where the churches were covered with gold. As a result, the greatest ambition of the Eastern Vikings was to attack and pillage Constantinople. Indeed, in

860, Askold and Dir launched a major seaborne attack against the Byzantine capital, whose defenders were taken by surprise. A Byzantine army had been fighting against the Arabs in the Middle East, and thus the defences of the city had been reduced. On 18 June, at sunset, some 200 Varangian ships sailed into the Bosphorus and started pillaging the suburbs of Constantinople. Encountering no opposition, the raiders then moved to the nearby Isles of the Princes, where they plundered the local dwellings and monasteries. After having pillaged without opposition for several days, the Varangians left Constantinople before any Byzantine military reinforcements could come to the aid of the city. Rurik continued to lead the Varangians until his death in 879. He was succeeded by Oleg, a capable warlord who acted as regent for his infant son, Igor. Oleg was an extremely capable military commander, and from the beginning of his rule he had only one main objective: preserving the unity of the Rus'. After attacking Constantinople, Askold and Dir had started to rule Kiev as an independent principality. This proved unacceptable for Novgorod, so Oleg led a large military expedition along the Dniepr between 880 and 882 in a bid to restore the unity of the Varangians. Smolensk and Lyubech were taken by Oleg's warriors before reaching Kiev, which then submitted and was transformed by Oleg into the capital of the Rus'. During the following years, the Varangian warlord created a centralized state and expanded his influence over an increasing number of Slav tribes, which were forced to pay tribute to the Scandinavians. For example, they had to provide large amounts of furs that the Varangians exchanged with the Byzantines in their markets. By 885, the subjugation of the Slavs had been practically completed and the Khazars had lost most of the influence they had previously exerted over Ukraine. The Rus' rapidly constructed a network of forts across their new domains and secured their control over the course of the major rivers. The new state of Kievan Rus' started to prosper and soon became a major power in Eastern Europe. The Varangians exported furs, beeswax, honey and slaves on a large scale. In addition, thanks to the strategic position of their territorial possessions, they connected the European markets with those of Central Asia and the Middle East. The Rus' princes and merchants became extremely rich, and an increasing demand for luxury goods developed in their lands.

The Byzantines tried to counter the ascendancy of the Varangians by forming an alliance with the Khazars and establishing a military presence in southern Crimea. It was the Khazars who supplied the Byzantines with the grain supplies that were vital for the survival of Constantinople's large population. These supplies came from Crimea and crossed the Black Sea before reaching the Byzantine ports. While adopting new military measures to resist the expansionism of the Rus', the Byzantines also tried to influence the Varangians from a cultural point of view by sending the missionary brothers Cyril and Methodius to Russia in 863. The two

Eastern Viking with helmet having nasal. (*Photo and copyright by Jomsborg Vikings Hird*)

Western Viking with chainmail and horn. (*Photo and copyright by Confraternita del Leone/Historia Viva*)

missionaries standardized the language of the Slavs by creating the Cyrillic alphabet and converted to Christianity large numbers of Slavs and Varangians. The increasing cultural influence of Byzantium over the Rus', however, did not change the political situation or stop the expansionism of the Varangians. Every year, Oleg of Kiev collected tributes from all the Slavs who were his subjects and assembled them on a flotilla of hundreds of boats that sailed down the Dniepr in order to reach the Black Sea. After being transported to Constantinople, the Varangian products were exchanged for Byzantine luxury goods such as silk, other fabrics, spices, wine and fruit. The Byzantines, however, were not particularly happy to exchange luxury goods for raw materials, and always tried to limit the commercial penetration of the Rus'. Under Oleg's rule, tensions between the Varangians and the Byzantines greatly increased, to the point that in 907, the Scandinavian monarch assembled an impressive fleet of 2,000 warships and attacked Constantinople. This time, however, the Byzantines were well prepared to receive the Varangians. The invaders found the gates of Constantinople closed and entry into the Bosphorus barred with iron chains. Oleg reacted quickly. Disembarking with his warriors on the nearest shore, he mounted wheels on his 2,000 warships to transform them into land vehicles. When the Varangians then surrounded the city walls with their boats, the terrified Byzantines quickly decided to come to terms with the attackers. Following these events, the Byzantines concluded two peace treaties with the Rus' (in 907 and 911) that had very positive terms for the Varangians. The latter were permitted to establish a colony of merchants inside Constantinople and were rewarded with tax-free trading privileges inside the Byzantine Empire.

Oleg died in 913 and was succeeded by Igor, the son of Rurik. The new Varangian monarch, despite the signing of the two treaties with the Byzantines, attacked the Byzantine Empire in 941 at the head of a large fleet of around 1,000 warships and 40,000 warriors. The Rus' disembarked on the northern coast of Asia Minor, in the very heart of the Byzantine Empire, where they pillaged the countryside with great violence. At that time, the Byzantine navy was fighting against the Arabs across the Mediterranean, so the Varangians could move in the Black Sea without encountering any opposition. The Byzantine defenders of Constantinople, however, were able to assemble a small naval force, with fifteen warships all equipped with 'Greek fire', a combustible mixture that was employed as a secret weapon by the Byzantines against enemy ships. When the Varangian fleet advanced against Constantinople, the Byzantines responded by using the Greek fire and destroyed several of the Rus' warships. This naval victory, however, was not a decisive one, since the raiders were able to disembark to pillage the hinterland of Constantinople. After four months of plundering in Asia Minor and Constantinople, the Varangians moved to Thrace,

Eastern Viking with pointed helmet and lamellar armour. (*Photo and copyright by Jomsborg Vikings Hird*)

Western Viking
with helmet having
nasal. (*Photo and
copyright by Brokkar
Lag*)

where a large Byzantine relief force reached their positions. By that time, the Byzantine navy had returned to the theatre of operations, and it launched a surprise attack against the Rus' in Thrace. During the ensuing naval battle, the Byzantines were able to prevail thanks to the use of the Greek fire, causing serious losses to their enemies. Igor, however, was able to escape with part of his fleet. In 944, the Varangians returned once more to Constantinople, this time with a larger fleet, with the intention of destroying the city. However, the Byzantines preferred to come to terms and a new peace treaty was signed in 945, which more or less confirmed the same terms that had been agreed with the previous treaties. Igor died shortly after signing the new treaty with the Byzantine Empire, being succeeded by his wife, Olga, who acted as regent for her infant son, Sviatoslav. The boy reached maturity in 963, and is remembered for his great military campaigns. Sviatoslav completed the conquest of the Khazar territories in Ukraine and even launched an invasion of the Balkans. The latter took place between 967 and 971 and saw the Rus' fighting against the 'First Bulgarian Empire', a large state that was created by the Bulgars, a nomadic people of the steppes, in the very heart of the Balkans. Within a few years, the Bulgars had become the most dangerous enemy of the Byzantines, who did not have the necessary military resources to retain control over the Balkans. In order to defeat the Bulgars, the Byzantines invited the Rus' to invade the territories of the newly born Bulgarian Empire from the north. The Varangians duly defeated the Bulgars, but it soon became clear that they would not stop north of the Byzantine lands. The two victorious allies soon turned against each other and a new conflict began. The Varangians were able to establish a protectorate over Bulgaria for several years, and in 970 a joint Varangian/Bulgarian army crossed Thrace before being defeated by the Byzantines at the Battle of Arcadiopolis. After this clash, the Byzantines were able to reconquer most of Bulgaria, after which the Rus' decided to abandon their plans of expansion in the Balkans. The Bulgarian Empire, meanwhile, ceased to exist as an autonomous state (at least for the moment). Sviatoslav died in 972, his death being followed by the outbreak of violent internecine conflicts between his three sons in order to determine the identity of the Varangians' new leader. In 980, Vladimir emerged victorious from the lengthy civil wars, and was the first to assume the title of 'Grand Prince of Kiev', playing a prominent part in the process that led to the final conversion of the Rus' to Christianity.

When Vladimir died, his son, Yaroslav, also had to struggle for power with his brothers. A new round of internal conflicts began, which ended only in 1019 when Yaroslav finally became Grand Prince of Kiev. Like his father before him, he had to go to Scandinavia in order to recruit an army of mercenaries to employ against his rivals. Yaroslav promulgated the first law code of his realm and constructed magnificent

Eastern Viking equipped with sabre and shield. (*Photo and copyright by Jomsborg Vikings Hird*)

Western Viking with leather helmet and double-handed Danish axe. (*Photo and copyright by Sjörvaldar Vikings*)

religious buildings in his important cities of Novgorod and Kiev. The death of Yaroslav in 1054 marked the beginning of the decline of the Rus', with his three sons starting to fight against each other to become supreme rulers of Kiev. At the same time, the southern portion of the Kievan Rus' started to be ravaged by the Cumans, a warlike people of the steppes who came from Central Asia. Taking advantage of the Varangians' internal divisions, the Cumans defeated them at the Battle of the Alta River in 1068. The civil conflicts that ravaged Russia during this period eventually led to the fall of the Kievan Rus', the various Varangian nobles starting to exert direct rule over their own lands and ceasing to respect the central authorities. Many minor princedoms emerged, which were constantly at war with each other. The internal struggles also had a religious character, since many Varangian aristocrats had perceived the adoption of the Christian faith as an imposition from Kiev. There was also a great rivalry existing between Novgorod and Kiev, two capitals that had contrasting interests and which were separated by an immense distance. After 1132, the last remnants of the Rus' former unity disappeared, the territory of Novgorod becoming officially independent and starting to be ruled as a republic. In 1169, the city of Kiev was raided by a coalition of Rus' aristocrats, thereafter ceasing to be a prominent political centre. By the end of the twelfth century, the territories that had been settled by the heirs of Rurik were fragmented into twelve major princedoms that were constantly at war against each other.

The Varangians are today considered as the real founders of Russia, since before their arrival the idea of a country stretching from the Baltic Sea to the Black Sea simply did not exist. Without their actions, the Slavs would have never been able to create a centralized state like Kievan Rus', which, despite its final political fragmentation, played a prominent role in the historical process that made Byzantine culture the dominant one in Eastern Europe. It was under the Princes of Kiev that the Varangians converted to Christianity, together with the Slavs. As has been made clear from the events described in this chapter, the Eastern Vikings were able to create a commercial empire that flourished for a long time and colonized an immense portion of Europe in just a few years. Bearing all this in mind, it is clear to see that their successes were equal in importance (if not superior) to those of the more well-known Western Vikings.

Chapter 13

The End of the Viking Age

Due to its proximity to the Holy Roman Empire, Denmark was the first area of Scandinavia where the Christian faith was introduced and a first form of a centralized kingdom was organized. During the period from 960–980, Harald Bluetooth, the second 'King of the Danes', unified most of the petty realms existing in Denmark into a single political entity, whose territory stretched from Jutland in the south to Scania in the north. Around the same time, Harald was visited by a German missionary who convinced him to convert to Christianity, together with his subjects. Despite these important changes, the Vikings of Denmark continued to act as raiders and conquerors during the closing decades of the tenth century, and with Cnut the Great they reached the peak of their power. After Cnut's death, a period of internal struggles began, causing the 'modernization' of the Kingdom of Denmark to be temporarily stopped. In 1080, a new monarch who would have played a fundamental role in the history of Denmark ascended the throne: Cnut IV. He was a very ambitious king, but also a very devout one. Cnut IV understood that the spreading of Christianity could help him in exerting effective control over his warlike aristocracy, so he supported the establishment of permanent religious institutions inside his realm. He was also the first Danish king who understood that the glorious and violent days of the Vikings were over: England was now a strong monarchy governed by a Norman royal house, and thus there was no realistic hope of conquering the British Isles. During his six-year reign, Cnut greatly limited the power of his aristocratic warlords by stifling them and by obliging them to respect the new laws introduced by the monarchy. He introduced a series of measures to discourage the organizing of piratical expeditions and boosted the authority of the monarch. Cnut arrogated to himself the ownership of common lands and the right to inherit possessions of foreign/kinless individuals when they died without heirs. In 1085, the king assembled a large fleet with the intention of attacking England. This time, however, the Danes who were to invade were peasant recruits and not Viking warriors. Due to a series of delays, the fleet was unable to leave Denmark as planned, which caused great malcontent among the many peasant soldiers who had been assembled for the invasion. They revolted against Cnut and obliged him to flee. The rebels gradually gained the upper hand in the struggle to secure power and

Western Viking warlord. (*Photo and copyright by Sjórvaldar Vikings*)

Western Viking warlord with fur cap. (*Photo and copyright by Sjórvaldar Vikings*)

killed the king. Due to his support for the Church and his violent death, Cnut was rapidly canonized and thus became an important figure in Danish culture. The death of Cnut IV and the failure of the expedition that he had planned effectively marked the end of the Viking Age for Denmark. During the following decades, the country became a part of Christian Europe and adopted the feudal system. Danish society had changed completely, with the once-warlike nobles who had organized Viking expeditions instead becoming feudal lords with large territorial possessions.

Norway had some form of monarchy from 872, when Harald Fairhair became king. It should be noted, however, that Harald and his early successors were just 'over-kings' who exerted nominal authority over the many Viking warlords who effectively had control of the country's fiords. This situation only started to change during the reign of Olaf Tryggvason, who became king in 995: he converted to Christianity before becoming monarch, and later tried to spread his new religion among the many pagans of Norway. This attempted conversion, however, caused great malcontent among his subjects and led to the outbreak of a civil war in 999. Most of the Norwegian nobles wanted to defend their pagan traditions and had no intention of accepting the presence of a strong monarchy that could damage their interests. Olaf was struggling to create a unified Norway by reducing the autonomy of the various petty kingdoms and regularizing the piratical activities of his subjects. His political plans were also considered potentially dangerous by the kings of Denmark and Sweden, who sided with the Norwegian rebel nobles during the civil war of 999. The internecine conflict ended in 1000 with the Battle of Svolder, which saw the defeat and death of Olaf Tryggvason. After the battle, Norway was divided into three parts: four of its districts were ceded to Sweden, one district to Denmark and the remainder retained their autonomy despite being organized as a Danish protectorate. The years between 1000 and 1040 were characterized for Norway by continuous civil wars, which included the participation of the Danes and Swedes on several occasions. After Cnut the Great started his military campaigns in England, the Norwegians began to resent Danish political influence over their kingdom, and gradually freed their country from the control of Denmark. Olaf Haraldsson was elected king in 1015 and soon started to expel the Swedes from his realm. In 1016, the decisive Battle of Nesjar was fought between the Norwegians and Swedes, which resulted in victory for Olaf. However, he soon also had to face the Danes after Cnut the Great completed his conquest of England. Incited by Cnut, who was now King of England as well as King of Denmark, many Norwegian nobles rebelled against Olaf, forcing him to leave Norway and go into exile. In 1030, the deposed monarch tried to regain control of his realm, but was defeated at the Battle of Stiklestad by a peasant army that was raised by the Norwegian aristocracy.

Until Cnut the Great's death in 1035, Norway remained under strong Danish political influence; in that year, however, the Norwegians rebelled against Denmark and elected Magnus Haraldsson (son of Olaf Haraldsson) as their king. Hostilities continued until 1040, when the new King of Norway and his Danish equivalent, Harthacnut, decided to come to terms: Denmark and Norway would remain two distinct realms until the death of one of them, when the survivor would unify the two countries under his rule. As a result of this, when Harthacnut died in 1042, Magnus

Eastern Viking warlord with fur cap. (*Photo and copyright by Sjórvaldar Vikings*)

Haraldsson became King of Denmark. He continued the policy of his father, Olaf, who had been canonized by the Church, since they both shared two main objectives: defeating paganism and reducing the power of the Norwegian nobles. In 1047, Magnus Haraldsson died and the temporary unity between Denmark and Norway was broken. In Norway, he was succeeded by Harald Hardrada, the last of the great

Nice examples of Viking sword, axe and scramasax dagger. (*Photo and copyright by Sjórvaldar Vikings*)

Viking monarchs. Harald was a half-brother of Magnus and had great ambitions. Between 1048 and 1064, he spent most of his time fighting against the Danes in an attempt to restore the union between Norway and Denmark. When his Scandinavian plans failed, Harald turned his attention to England, launching an invasion in 1066. After Harald Hardrada's death at Stamford Bridge, Norway was ruled by his two sons, Magnus and Olaf, until 1093. During this period, the Church was permitted to establish a permanent presence in Norway and an increasing number of Norwegians converted to Christianity. At the same time, the power of the monarchy was greatly increased, with the various Viking warlords forced to respect the new laws that were promulgated by King Olaf III. The political and social transformation of the Kingdom of Norway was completed by Olaf's son, Magnus Barefoot, who reigned during the period 1093–1103 and introduced a form of proto-feudalism. Under his rule, the Viking Age also came to an end in Norway.

The first monarch in the history of Sweden was Eric the Victorious (reigned 970–995), who fought against the King of Denmark, Sweyn Forkbeard, in order to secure the autonomy of his domains. Until 970, Sweden did not exist as an independent realm, with the Swedish Vikings living under the political influence of Denmark. Eric's son and successor, Olof, initially had to accept the overlordship of Sweyn Forkbeard, and even fought at the latter's side against the Norwegians in 1000. Thanks to their alliance with the Kingdom of Denmark, the Swedes obtained control over several districts of Norway and their monarchy became a stable institution. Soon after the Kingdom of Norway regained its autonomy from Denmark in 1015, however, a new war broke out between the Norwegians and the Swedes. This did not last long, and ended with success for the Kingdom of Sweden, which annexed the Norwegian districts of Jamtland and Halsingland. As the Swedish monarchs, starting from Olof, had great difficulties in convincing their subjects to become Christians, Sweden was the last of the Scandinavian countries to adopt the new religion. Between 1022 and 1060, Sweden was ruled by Olof's two sons, Anund Jacob and Edmund. Anund was a fierce enemy of Cnut the Great and tried to break up the temporary union that was formed between Denmark and Norway. In 1026, however, he and his allies were defeated at the Battle of Helgea. Edmund was the first Swedish monarch to plan to colonize Finland, and spent most of his reign trying to establish a 'balance of power' in the Scandinavian world. For example, he determined the limits for the first time of the border between Denmark and Sweden by collaborating with the Danish king, Sweyn Estridsen. A new royal family, the House of Stenkil, assumed control over the Kingdom of Sweden in 1060. Its first member, Stenkil, fought a brief but bloody war against Harald Hardrada in order to support the King of Denmark, Sweyn Estridsen. After Stenkil's death in 1066, Sweden entered a regressive historical phase, with the kings who followed him unable to increase the power of the central government, so the realm continued to be dominated by the various local warlords. Around 1100, under the rule of Inge the Elder, the majority of the Swedish population converted to Christianity and the strength of the central government was increased. The expeditions of the Varangians directed towards Russia then became very sporadic, and – after a brief new conflict – a stable peace treaty was signed between the Kingdoms of Norway and Sweden.

By 1100, the Norse pirates and raiders who had been given the name of Vikings no longer existed, since their Scandinavian homeland had completely changed from a political and social point of view. It should be noted, however, that some military institutions created by the Vikings continued to survive well after their disappearance. The most famous and important of these was without doubt the famous Varangian Guard, a Scandinavian military unit that was part of the Byzantine Army for a long time. After the end of hostilities between the Rus' and the Byzantines in 971, the diplomatic relations between Constantinople and Kiev improved a lot, partly because some of the Varangian princes married female members of the Byzantine imperial

Viking sword. (*Photo and copyright by Jomsborg Vikings Hird*)

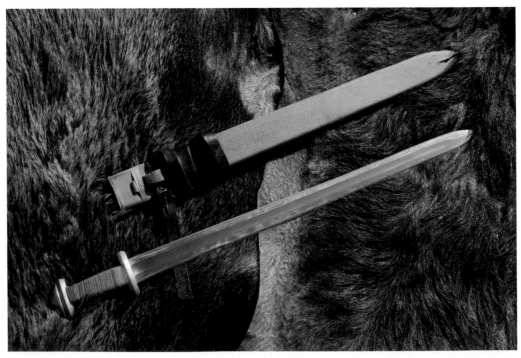

Viking sword. (*Photo and copyright by Jomsborg Vikings Hird*)

family. By that time, the Byzantine Empire was heavily involved in a series of military theatres and thus had great difficulties in deploying substantial numbers of soldiers on its vast Balkan frontier. Trying to solve this problem, the Byzantine kings decided to recruit increasing numbers of Rus' mercenaries who could serve as part of their military forces. The Varangians, like all the Vikings, were eager to fight for money and were among the most professional fighters of their age. Consequently, from 970 onwards, substantial numbers of Rus' mercenaries could be found in the Byzantine Army. These were mostly deployed across the Balkans, where their main task was to counter the incursions of the nomadic peoples that took place in that part of the empire. In 987, a bloody civil war broke out inside Byzantine territory, which forced Emperor Basil II to ask for help from the Prince of Kiev, Vladimir the Great. Prince Vladimir responded to the call, confirming the alliance existing between Kiev and Constantinople, and sent a contingent of 6,000 elite warriors, who were chosen from the best Rus' fighters. The Varangians serving under Basil II played a prominent role during the Byzantine civil war and helped secured victory for their master. During the period from 988–999, they took part in all the military campaigns that were fought by the Byzantine Army, into which they were officially absorbed. Serving in Constantinople was a dream for the Rus', who soon learned how to live according to the luxurious lifestyle of the Byzantines; they were paid very well by the emperor and were highly respected by their imperial commanders. Over time, the Byzantine kings started to rely on these courageous and audacious foreigners for their personal defence: the Varangians were not involved (at least initially) in the political machinations of Constantinople, and thus – especially in the case of civil war – they would always remain loyal to their emperor (i.e. the person who paid them).

In 1000, the Byzantines decided to transform the Rus' warriors into an elite corps of the Imperial Guard, and the old veterans from Kiev were organized as the legendary Varangian Guard. This unit soon became famous for its loyalty and discipline. They were all armed with axes, and their stature was impressive by Byzantine standards. The Varangians took part in all the major campaigns that were fought by the Byzantine Army, in every corner of the empire. They always distinguished themselves, and defeated every kind of enemy that they encountered on the battlefield. Service in the Varangian Guard eventually started to become a sort of 'military apprenticeship' for young Viking aristocrats who wanted to travel around the Mediterranean and European world in their early years and to learn the most advanced military practices of the age. Around 1040, Harald Hardrada, the future King of Norway, served in the elite corps and participated in several campaigns under the orders of the Byzantine emperor. In 1071, the Varangian Guard took part in the bloody Battle of Manzikert, which saw the crushing defeat of the Byzantine Army by the Seljuk Turks. Many of the original Rus' warriors died in the clash, being killed from distance by the arrows of the Turkish mounted archers. After Manzikert, the Byzantine Empire ceased to be a major military power in Europe, and the internal composition of the Varangian Guard changed considerably, with many of the fallen Scandinavians substituted with Saxon professional soldiers who had left England after Hastings and the Norman Conquest and were in search of employment. Until Manzikert, the Varangian Guard consisted of around 6,000 warriors, but after the battle, this figure was reduced by half to just 3,000 men. The elite corps, which lost most of its original Scandinavian character after 1071, continued to exist as part of the Imperial Guard until 1204, when the city of Constantinople was conquered by the Western Europeans during the Fourth Crusade.

As we have seen in an earlier chapter, the Viking presence in Ireland and some peripheral areas of Scotland was very significant and led to the birth of the Norse-Gaels (i.e. individuals of mixed Scandinavian and Gael descent). These were well integrated into the Gaelic world but retained the military traditions of their Viking ancestors, such as the use of axes on the battlefield. Over time, the Norse-Gaels started to be employed as mercenary warriors by several Irish and Scottish nobles, who admired their great military capabilities. As a result, many decades after the end of the Viking Age, some professional warriors continued to fight in the Scandinavian way on the soil of the British Isles. These fierce mercenaries were commonly known as Gallowglasses, using a term that meant 'foreign warriors'. The Norse-Gael fighters came from the areas of Ireland that had been settled by the Vikings, but also – more notably – from the territories of the former Kingdom of the Isles and the western coastline of Scotland. The Gallowglasses were employed on a large scale by the Irish warlords from 1260 and took part in all the most important conflicts that were fought in Ireland. Coming from Scotland and being professional fighters, they were much more reliable than most of the Irish warriors. Furthermore, they fought with deadly axes like their Viking ancestors, and could therefore be used as a sort of 'psychological' weapon. Most of the early Gallowglasses came from the Kingdom of the Isles and were professional soldiers in search of new employment, their homeland having been annexed by Scotland. Initially, the mercenary Norse-Gael soldiers were simply paid with sums of money, but they later started to be given a piece of land in exchange for their military services. As a result, by the time the English tried to conquer Ireland, many Gallowglasses had already settled on Irish territory and were entitled to receive supplies from the local communities. During the Middle Ages, the Norse-Gael mercenaries became a distinct component of Irish society and played a prominent role in slowing down the English conquest of the island. They served with distinction on many occasions, being the best heavy infantry that was available

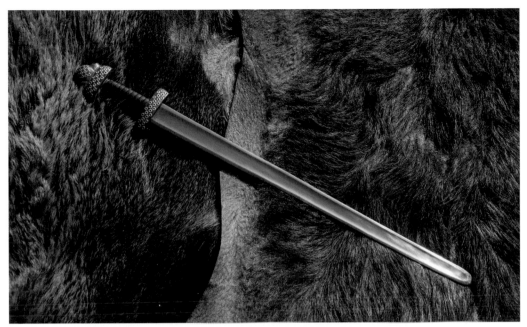

Viking sword. (*Photo and copyright by Jomsborg Vikings Hird*)

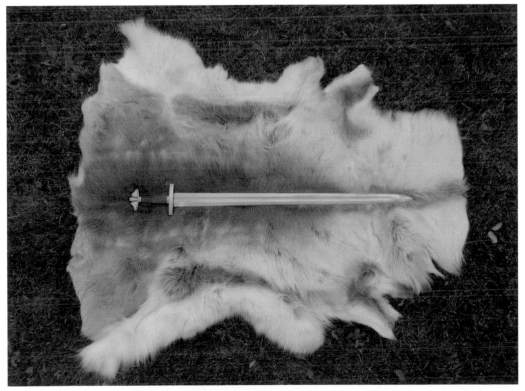

Viking sword. (*Photo and copyright by Sjórvaldar Vikings*)

in Ireland. Most of the other Irish infantrymen were lightly equipped, while the Irish aristocrats (who were rich enough to buy heavy armour) preferred fighting as cavalrymen. Being foreigners, the Gallowglasses were often employed as bodyguards by the Irish nobles, so could exert a considerable political influence. They continued to be a fundamental component of Irish armies until the beginning of the seventeenth century, when the final English conquest of Ireland and the diffusion of gunpowder weapons determined their decline. As shown by the history of the Gallowglasses, the Viking heritage in the British Isles was much more important and durable than one could imagine. Indeed, during the Viking Age, most of Europe had to deal – in one way or in another – with the fierce warriors of Scandinavia.

Chapter 14

Viking Military Organization

The Scandinavian society of the Viking Age consisted of three main classes: the *jarls* or nobles, the *karls* or freemen and the *praell* or slaves. The *jarls* were distinguished by their wealth, which was measured according to their personal possessions: estates, ships and goods. In addition, the power of the *jarls* was determined by the number of retainers who were under their orders. Thanks to their large territorial possessions, the Viking nobles could exert their influence over significant numbers of *karls*. Their main task was to keep order in their estates as well as to guarantee prosperity for their retainers by organizing piratical expeditions across the sea. Most of the *jarls*, especially in Norway, controlled a naval base (usually located in a fiord), where their warships were built and repaired. The social position of *jarl* was hereditary, but it was not uncommon to see a *karl* becoming a noble: by conducting successful raids or by serving as a well-paid mercenary, a common freeman could become rich enough to improve his social condition. The vast majority of the Vikings were *karls*, i.e. freemen who owned some lands and earned their living as farmers. Their families lived in small clusters of just three or four buildings, and thus no large towns or cities existed in Viking Scandinavia. Each cluster usually comprised a 'longhouse', which was the common property of the whole community, plus some barns and workshops. Family ties were particularly important and determined the social position of an individual, together with his personal wealth. The *praell* were slaves captured during incursions or bondsmen; they worked in the estates of the *jarls* or the farms of the *karls*, being treated as any other material possession. The power of a noble, for example, was also determined by the number of slaves he owned. If a Viking of any social class was unable to pay his debts, he was obliged to become a bondsman and was forced to work for his 'master' until the debt was paid. The *jarls* usually had significant numbers of bondsmen, who were forced to follow their masters during military expeditions.

The social organization described above determined the structure of Viking military forces, which had a nucleus represented by the *hird* or 'retinue'. Each *jarl* had his own *hird* of professional warriors, who were paid for their services and had sworn their allegiance to the *jarl*. The *hirdsmen* were maintained by their noble and came from the social class of the *karls*; most of the Viking aristocrats had a *hird* of

Viking scramasax dagger. (*Photo and copyright by Sjórvaldar Vikings*)

between sixty and 120 warriors, according to their personal wealth and power. Each *hird* was commanded by an 'officer' known as a *hersir*, who generally was a rich *karl* aspiring to become an aristocratic landowner. The *hersirs* were the real backbone of the Viking fighting forces, since they were chosen from their own community because of their combat capabilities as well as their personal influence. When a *jarl*

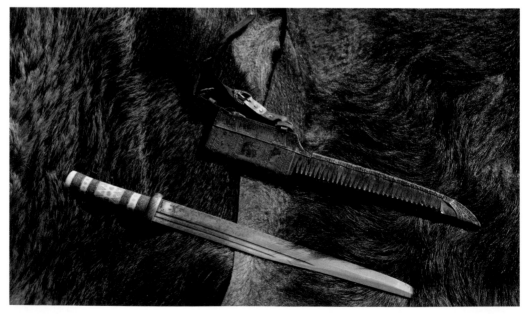

Viking knife. (*Photo and copyright by Jomsborg Vikings Hird*)

decided to conduct an expedition overseas, it was the *hersirs* who organized the raid from a practical point of view. Each of these military commanders was at the head of some fifteen to twenty-five *hirdsmen*, so in each retinue there were between four and eight *hersirs*. In 885, Harald Fairhair, King of Norway, decreed that each *jarl* should have at least eighty *hirdsmen* and four *hersirs* under his command. No central military forces existed, as even the kings had to count on the loyalty of their *jarls* in order to raise armies. Each monarch, however, had his own elite retinue like any other Scandinavian noble. Harald Hardrada, for example, had a royal *hird* of 120 warriors; Olaf III of Norway (reigned 1068–1093) doubled this and increased the number of his *hirdsmen* to 240. In later times, the 'long hundred' – consisting of 120 warriors – became the standard organizational unit of the Viking military forces. Each 'company' of 120 men was divided into four sub-units, with thirty warriors each; these could in turn be divided into three small groups of ten fighters. Each sub-unit was commanded by a *hersir*, so there were four 'officers' in each company. Each *hird* also had two members who enjoyed elite status: the *stallari* and the *merkismadr*. The former acted as a sort of 'field marshal' and was a warrior of great experience, while the latter acted as the standard-bearer of his retinue. The internal composition of the *hirds* eventually became more complex, since a new category of fighters appeared: these were the *gestir*, free men who did not own land and received only half the pay of a normal *hirdsman*. The *gestir* only appeared in Viking armies from the early decades of the ninth century. Due to their lower social position, they did not serve as heavy infantrymen like the *hirdsmen* but as light infantrymen.

The *hirdsmen* provided the bulk of the Viking fighting forces and were frequently paid with the money that was extorted from foreign communities with the danegeld. They, in addition, divided the booty of the incursions together with their *jarls*. The *jarls* understood that the only way to gain the loyalty of a professional warrior was to pay him with regularity and to conduct successful piratical incursions that could lead to the capture of substantial booties. To further maintain the support of the *hirdsmen*, the *jarls* provided gifts to their men; these had both a symbolic and a material value, being weapons or gold rings on most occasions. A valiant fighter could also receive some special 'prizes', for example a piece of land. The Vikings considered courage in battle as the most important virtue that a man could have, and thus sometimes even freed their slaves if they showed great valour in combat. The Scandinavian society of the Viking Age was mostly an agricultural one, since most of the free men were farmers who produced corn and had cattle. Between ploughing and harvest time, the *karls* took part in the commercial/piratical expeditions organized by their nobles. Consequently, it would be wrong to consider plundering as the only or main component of the Viking economy. The *hersirs* played a prominent role in the Scandinavian military organization, since they were farmers like the men under their command but also had superior military skills. On most occasions, the twenty-five to thirty-five warriors commanded by a *hersir* corresponded to the crew of a warship, and thus the *hersir* was also the captain of their vessel. Providing gifts and promising booty were the only ways for a *hersir* to raise an effective war band comprising at least thirty fighters. The small groups of warriors commanded by a *hersir* were characterized by the existence of a special relationship between their members, since all the fighters of a retinue were 'brother-in-arms' and had sworn loyalty to their *jarl* over the hilt of their sword. The military system based on the *hird* was common to the entire Viking world, with the only difference that the retinues of the Varangians (the Eastern Vikings) were known as *druzhinas*. As mentioned above, during the last phase of the Viking Age, the traditional *hirdsmen* started to be supported by some *gestir* or 'guests', free men of lower social status who served as light infantrymen. These also performed a series of auxiliary roles such as policing the countryside or collecting taxes from their *jarl's* subjects.

The military system based on retinues or war bands was used to assemble the troops that were needed for overseas expeditions. In case of foreign attack against their homeland, however, the Vikings employed a different system of mobilization that was known as *leidang*. According to this system, each *jarl* was obliged to provide ships and crews at his own expense if these were needed by his king. Over time, the *leidang* also started to be used to organize massive offensive operations, such as invasions of a foreign land, and thus partly lost its initial defensive nature. The territories of the three Scandinavian kingdoms were all divided into districts, each of which, according to its population and economic capabilities, had to provide and maintain a certain number of warships that were to serve under command of the central authorities when needed. The *leidang* or 'naval conscription' system existed in all the Scandinavian countries, but each realm had its own peculiarities. In Denmark, territory was divided into *skipen* or ship-districts, each of which was to provide a warship; each district, in turn, was divided into harbour-districts that were to provide one sailor/warrior each. Usually, naval conscription worked according to a rotation system, and thus the various ship-districts had to provide their vessel only every four years. In Norway, however, territory was divided into counties and these were in turn divided into coastal districts, each of which was to provide a warship and forty crewmen in case of mobilization. The territory of Sweden was divided into six regions; five of these had no outlet to the sea and were divided into territorial units known as 'hundreds', while the remaining one (comprising the entire coastline of the country) was divided into ship-districts. Each of the hundreds and the ship-districts was to provide four warships and 100 sailors/warriors (Swedish ships were smaller than the Danish/Norwegian ones and had crews of twenty-five rowers). The conscript forces were responsible for homeland defence and consequently also performed auxiliary

Viking double-handed axe. (*Photo and copyright by Jomsborg Vikings Hird*)

Blade of a double-handed axe. (*Photo and copyright by Jomsborg Vikings Hird*)

functions like patrolling the coastline and transmitting warnings with beacon-chains. When the power of the Scandinavian kings became more significant, from the early decades of the eleventh century, the naval conscription system began to be employed in order to muster large invasion forces. The army that Harald Hardrada led to England in 1066, for example, mostly consisted of conscript warriors rather than *hirds*. Nevertheless, these 'general' mobilizations never involved all the able-bodied free men of a country: usually, only one or two out of every three individuals were called to serve at a time, since a substantial labour force had to remain at home in order to work in the fields. Those men who were not mobilized also had to work in the fields of the warriors who had been called to serve. A full mobilization (*full-leidang*) was quite rare to see, since on most occasions the kings preferred to employ a half mobilization (*half-leidang*). It should be remembered that the conscript warships were usually available for royal service only for short periods of two to four months.

Over the passing years, an increasing number of Viking warriors started to sell their military services to the various *jarls* as professional mercenaries. These became increasingly important in the Viking military system from the closing decades of the tenth century and were frequently organized into 'brotherhoods' that had a distinct pagan nature. The most famous of these mercenary groups was that of the *Jomsvikings*, who fought for any Viking leader who was rich enough to pay them. The *Jomsvikings* had their main base at Jomsborg, on the southern coast of the Baltic Sea, from where they organized their expeditions. The senior members of the brotherhood were extremely selective in deciding whom to admit to their mercenary organization: membership was restricted to warriors of proven valour aged 18–50, who had to fight a duel with one of the *Jomsvikings* in order to show their combat abilities. All the components of the brotherhood had to respect a strict code of discipline, which was based on severe punishments. Blood feuds between members of the group were prohibited, and all *Jomsvikings* were forbidden to flee from the battlefield. All captured spoils were to be equally distributed among the entire brotherhood, and no member was permitted to leave the stronghold of Jomsborg for more than three days. The *Jomsvikings* were probably created by Harald Bluetooth (King of Denmark from 958–986) and became increasingly powerful; according to contemporary sources, at the height of their power they could deploy a total of thirty warships. In 984, the *Jomsvikings* tried to conquer Sweden for one of their leaders but were defeated by Eric the Strong, the first King of Sweden. Two years later, they attacked Norway, always being in search of a realm to conquer, but also on this occasion they were defeated. The twin defeats of 984 and 986 marked the beginning of the decline for the *Jomsvikings*, who were now perceived as a menace rather than a resource by the Scandinavian monarchs who had previously employed them. By the 980s, however, the mercenary brotherhood was strong enough to threaten the stability

Viking axe. (*Photo and copyright by Jomsborg Vikings Hird*)

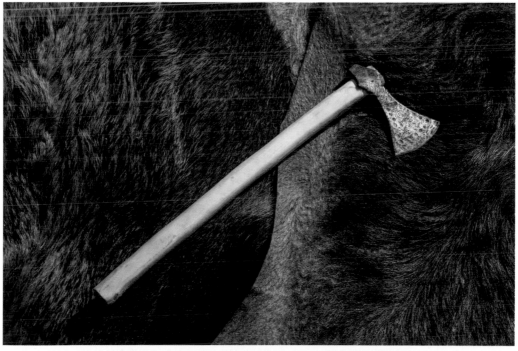

Viking axe. (*Photo and copyright by Jomsborg Vikings Hird*)

of the Scandinavian realms. In addition, the *Jomsvikings* were the last and fiercest defenders of Viking paganism. Considering them to be a potential threat for the 'modernization' of his kingdom, Magnus I of Norway decided to attack them in 1043. As a result, Jomsborg was destroyed by Magnus' forces and most of the *Jomsvikings* were killed.

The Scandinavian military forces of the Viking Age also included a special category of elite warriors, the *Berserkers*. These were part of religious brotherhoods that had a distinct military character and were well known for their capacity of fighting with trance-like fury. The *Berserkers* honoured wild animals that were central to the pagan religion of the Norse and tried to emulate their combat skills; for this reason, they wore no armour and covered their bodies just with the skin of the animal that they honoured. The same term 'Berserker' means 'bear-shirt', because these elite warriors used to wear coats made out of a bear's skin. The traditions related to the *Berserkers* were extremely ancient and originated from the hunts of the early Scandinavian communities. Three main animal cults were practised by the Vikings: that of the bear, the wolf and the wild boar. Bear-warriors, wolf-warriors and boar-warriors all had some fundamental characteristics in common: in battle they were subject to fits of frenzy, howled like wild beasts, foamed at the mouth and gnawed the iron rim of their shields. According to popular belief, during these frenzied attacks, they were immune to steel and fire. While fighting against the enemy, the *Berserkers* assumed the combat capabilities of the animal they honoured, and were thus said to have a supernatural tendency to kill. Contemporary Scandinavian sources use the expression 'to go berserk' to indicate the moment in which these warriors 'changed form' and entered a state of wild fury. We don't know how the *Berserkers* were able to enter such a trancelike state during battle, but they were probably a mixture of psychopaths and sufferers from paranoia who were sent to the front line of battle in order to terrorize the enemy. Judging from contemporary sources, they were not numerous, but their appearance on the battlefield could decide the outcome of a clash: they had the physical strength of madmen and were impervious to pain. Before the spreading of Christianity, the *Berserkers* were part of the pagan kings' bodyguards and were highly prized as a result of their 'supernatural' powers. Harald Fairhair and several other Viking kings employed them as shock troops, until paganism was gradually banished from Scandinavia. According to the latest research, it is possible that some of the *Berserkers* could reach hysteria by performing a ritualistic process known as *effektnummer* that included shield-biting and animalistic howling.

Naval warfare was a fundamental component of the Viking world: ships were not only a means of transport, but also a symbol of power, since control of the sea routes was a key element behind the success of a Viking community. Before the advent of sail, the Norse people employed simple rowing ships that could navigate only

Viking heavy spear. (This replica is blunted for re-enactment use; the real thing would have had a finely honed point.) (*Photo and copyright by Jomsborg Vikings Hird*)

Point of a Viking heavy spear. (*Photo and copyright by Jomsborg Vikings Hird*)

along the coastline. With the so-called 'Sail Revolution' of the early Viking Age, new models of ships were developed and the Scandinavians could set out over the open sea. Manufacturing large quantities of sail was a real challenge for medieval communities, since spinning and weaving wool to make sails required important economic resources and a consistent labour force. Nevertheless, the advantages given by the introduction of sail were so significant that the Norse communities soon changed their shipbuilding practices in order to mount sails on their vessels. This revolution was made possible by the invention of the keel, which permitted the development of the famous longship. The Scandinavian clinker-built wooden vessels with keel, oars and sail were going to conquer the known world: they could maintain an average speed of 4–5 knots under oars and a maximum speed of 20 knots under sail, which was incredible for the standards of the time. The longships could be operated in very shallow waters due to their flat keel, and thus were perfect to sail on rivers; in addition, they could be easily landed on sloping beaches. Their rudder, which reached far below the keel, could be pulled up to avoid damaging it on the seabed; Viking ships could therefore be moved out of reach of enemy ships, which were unable to follow them into shallow waters. The longships had several superior technological features which made them extremely resistant; for example, they had a shock-absorbing inlay between the bow and the keel (which could be easily removed if damaged). The shallow keel was also perfect to transport horses, something that William the Conqueror used to his advantage during the 1066 invasion of England. The great manoeuvrability and flexibility of the Viking ships made them reliable and seaworthy in every climatic condition. Being lighter and faster than enemy vessels, the longships were practically impossible to defeat during sea battles and could be deployed in different tactical formations according to circumstances. The combination of oars and sail gave the Vikings an incredible superiority over their enemies. Scandinavian ships belonged to three main categories: *knarrs* or cargo ships (bigger and broader vessels specifically designed for transporting goods and heavy freight), *karvs* or barges (small boats used for sailing between islands and skerries) and longships. The latter had a steering oar at the starboard side of the aft stem, a big rectangular sail and several fixed thwarts above the deck. The Viking longships were also known as *drakkar* or *dreki*, since they frequently had carvings of animal heads (most notably of dragons/*dreki*) at the stem. These carved heads were usually only mounted for combat and were painted with bright colours. Ships employed for military service were also easy to recognize thanks to the presence of shields hanging along their sides (which were attached to a rope that was tied to the rim of the vessel). These shields were part of the ship's fittings and not of the rowers' personal equipment, being used for protection from enemy arrows.

Chapter 15

Viking Military Equipment and Tactics

The Vikings were famous for the high quality of their weapons, which had a specific social function in Scandinavia during the early Middle Ages: bearing arms was both a right and a duty of the freemen and distinguished them from slaves. As a result, weapons were status symbols, and their quality and ornamentation reflected the economic capabilities of their owner. Most of the Viking warriors gave their weapons a name and had a special relationship with them, as they also acted like amulets protecting them from danger and evil and their symbolism was strongly linked to the very soul of their owner. Elegant shapes and rich ornamentations were typical of the aristocrats' weaponry, but most of the middle-class warriors also had no hesitation in spending large sums of their money in order to have the best arms. In Viking Scandinavia, the processes of forging and tempering weapons were performed by specialized craftsmen and were surrounded by a web of myth: use of the best materials and control of the temperatures during the various production phases were key factors behind the creation of an effective weapon. Viking arms were often decorated with symbols that had a religious or cultural meaning, which were reproduced as patterns laid into the iron during forging and became visible when the external surface of the weapon was polished and etched. A good sword blade had to be flexible but should not be easily broken, while the edge had to keep its sharpness for as long as possible. These main characteristics were obtained by placing hard steel on the sword's edge and soft iron along the middle of the blade. Producing a sword of good quality was an extremely long process, which had many phases: forging, folding, hammering and forging again. Reworking steel and iron at high temperatures rendered them homogenous and thus reduced the risk of the weapon shattering under the strain of use. The production of axes was less complex than that of swords, since iron of lower quality could be used to cast their middle part.

The most iconic offensive weapon of the Vikings is the axe, which was the arm of the freemen. It originally developed from the tool that was employed for work in the woods, which was quite massive. Around 950, however, working axes and battle axes became two distinct objects, with the former starting to be lighter and narrower. In combat, the Vikings employed their axes mostly to break enemy lines like 'shield-smashers', but it is important to bear in mind that three different kinds of axe were produced and that each of these had distinctive peculiarities: narrow-bladed axes, broad-bladed axes and bearded axes. Narrow-bladed axes had a blade length of 5–10cm and were mostly employed as working tools; those having a two-handed wooden shaft were known as *boloks* and were used for felling trees. The narrow-bladed axe was not specifically designed for combat use, but since it was the only axe owned by many of the poorest freemen it was not uncommon to see it on the battlefield. Broad-bladed axes had a blade length of 20–30 cm and were specifically designed for combat use, with a head that could be L-shaped or M-shaped. The blade was thin but wide and had pronounced 'horns' at both the toe and the heel of the bit. These characteristics were also common to the narrow-bladed axes, but the latter were not as thin as the battle axes. L-shaped axes tended to be smaller and had the toe of the bit swept forward for superior shearing capability. M-shaped axes, meanwhile, were bigger and had a more symmetrical toe and heel. Most of the battle axes were built with wrought iron but had a reinforced bit made of carbon steel that was placed near the edge in order to have a devastating cutting capability. The average weight of a Viking battle axe was 1.5kg, while the wooden haft had a standard length of 1–1.5 metres and was linked to the head with a cap that protected the edge of the haft that went into the metal head from the rigours of combat. On most occasions, the haft was made from ash or oak. Both the narrow-bladed axe and the broad-bladed axe were employed as double-handed weapons and were not designed for throwing, while the bearded axe or *skeggox* was single-handed and mostly employed as a throwing weapon. Its name derived from the hook or 'beard', i.e. the lower portion of the head's bit that extended the cutting edge below the width of the butt (providing a wide cutting surface while keeping the overall weight of the weapon low). The peculiar design of the bearded axe allowed its user to grip the haft directly behind the head, something that was of great use when throwing the weapon.

Swords, which were much more expensive and complex to produce than axes, were generally used only by the most prominent warriors. The Viking sword was a single-handed weapon that was designed to leave the warrior's other hand free in order to hold the shield. When employing two-handed axes, Viking warriors had to carry their shields on the back. Scandinavian swords could be single-handed or double-handed (the latter being much more common than the former). Their hilt consisted of three parts: back-hilt, grip and fore-hilt. Sometimes the latter was made up of two parts, the hindmost of which was commonly known as the pommel. Most of the hilts were made of iron, but sometimes they could be of bronze. The total length of a Viking sword was generally 90–95cm, while the average length of the blade was 75–80cm. Blades were some 5–6cm wide and their weight was restricted towards the point, which was made possible by tapering the blades both in breadth and thickness. As a result, blade thickness was 6mm near the hilt and 2mm at the point of the sword. To further reduce the weight, and also to increase flexibility, a groove was

Viking light spear. (*Photo and copyright by Jomsborg Vikings Hird*)

Point of a Viking light spear. (*Photo and copyright by Jomsborg Vikings Hird*)

Viking light javelin. (*Photo and copyright by Jomsborg Vikings Hird*)

forged and ground out along the middle of the blade. The centre of gravity of the weapon was near the hilt, which made it quite easy to handle in combat. Many Viking swords, especially those belonging to the richest individuals, had decorative inscriptions on the blade and decorated hilts. All swords were carried in leather-bound wooden scabbards that were suspended from a strap across the right shoulder. Like the scabbard, the hilt was also made of an organic material, such as horn or antler. Swords had such an important symbolic and material value for the Vikings that they were usually passed from one generation to another. Many prominent warlords even chose to be buried together with their personal sword. Most of these buried swords had their blade bent in order to deter any robbers from violating the burials to steal such costly weapons.

The spear was the weapon of the poorer warriors in the Viking world, unlike the sword that was the weapon of the rich and the axe that was the weapon of the middle-class. As the spear was very easy to produce, it was carried by the great majority of the common fighters. Scandinavian spears were produced in two main versions: throwing spears and thrusting spears. The heads of the throwing spears had an average length of 20cm, while those of the thrusting spears had a standard length of 70cm. Spear heads consisted of two parts: the blade and the socket. The wooden shaft was fixed into the socket with one or two nails; Viking spears could sometimes

Point of a Viking light javelin. (*Photo and copyright by Jomsborg Vikings Hird*)

Viking heavy javelin. (*Photo and copyright by Jomsborg Vikings Hird*)

Point of a Viking heavy javelin. (*Photo and copyright by Jomsborg Vikings Hird*)

also have two projections on the side of the socket that were known as 'wings', which were used to make it more easy to remove the spear from enemy shields. Occasionally, the back end of the shaft was capped with a metal ferrule to add strength to the spear. Spear blades could be of two different kinds. The first and older model of blade was forged with a herringbone pattern along the middle, and had curved edges; it blended inconspicuously into the socket. The newer type of blade tended towards a square internal cross-section and was decorated with longitudinal grooves. This model of blade also had nearly straight edges (which ended in an angle at the base) and a marked narrowing as it merged into the socket. The latter was round in cross-section and was decorated with inlaid precious metal. Wings were very common on the older model and quite rare on the newer spears. The wings had another important practical function in addition to that of making easier the extraction of the spear from enemy shields: they could be used for hooking onto the edge of an enemy shield and thus opening the way for a strike. The wooden shaft of the thrusting spear (generally some 2.5–3 metres) was longer than that of the throwing spear (1.5 metres). The diameter of all shafts was about 2.5cm, and sometimes narrowed away from the point. Throwing spears were less popular with Viking fighters than thrusting ones.

In addition to their axes, swords and spears, the Viking warriors sometimes also carried a long battle knife known as a *sax*. This was single-bladed, having a curved back and a straight edge. Its total length was between 70 and 90cm, which made it comparable to smaller swords. The handle of a *sax* was some 15–25cm long and was made of wood. This short weapon was carried across the front of the lower abdomen, hung horizontally from the warrior's belt. The cutting edge faced upward, with the handle conveniently placed for the user's right hand. The *sax* was copied by the Vikings from the Saxons, and thus was popular among the Western Vikings. The Varangians, meanwhile, had shorter battle knives, the back and edge of which were both straight.

Bows were much more popular among Viking warriors than is generally thought. They were employed for both hunting and warfare, and thus were a common object that could be found in most Scandinavian houses. Viking bows could be made from yew, ash or elm. They had a draw force of 100lb and an effective range of 200 metres. From a technical point of view they should be classed as longbows, since they were made from a single piece of wood. The overall height of a Viking bow generally corresponded to that of its user. When not in use, a Scandinavian bow was almost straight; when strung, it was nearly D-shaped in cross-section. Arrowheads could be of three different kinds: blade-shaped, spike-shaped and chisel-shaped. The second model was that specifically designed for use in combat, while the other two were also employed for hunting. Each arrowhead was fixed with a tang to its shaft; the latter was made of wood, had feathers applied on the back and was about 65–75cm long.

Viking wooden bow. (*Photo and copyright by Jomsborg Vikings Hird*)

Front of a
Viking round
shield. (*Photo
and copyright
by Jomsborg
Vikings Hird*)

Back of a
Viking round
shield. (*Photo
and copyright
by Jomsborg
Vikings Hird*)

The most important component of a Viking warrior's defensive panoply was his shield, which had a distinctive round shape and was quite flat, having a hole in the middle where a wooden carrying handle was mounted crossways on the inside. A dome of plate iron, the boss, was nailed over the hole on the outside in order to protect the hand. Viking shields had a diameter of 80–95cm and were made up of seven or eight planks glued together, edge to edge, in order to form a single plate. The thickness of the planks was 7–8mm near the middle of the shield, tapering to 5–6mm near the edge. A layer of rawhide was glued onto the whole of the shield's front and back, being held in position by stitch holes that were placed round the edge, where a band of rawhide was folded round and sewn for reinforcement. The presence of the rawhide reduced the risk of the wood splitting and helped in stopping enemy arrows. Pine and spruce softwoods were usually chosen to create shields. Bosses could have a notched edge or a crenellated metal band set over the edge. Viking shields were frequently reinforced with an iron strip around the rim, which was particularly useful during hand-to-hand fighting. Most of the round shields were painted in a single colour, but some were decorated with specific designs. Simple crosses and derivations of sun wheels were the most common designs, together with sacred animals and creatures such as dragons. The average weight of a Viking shield was 7kg. When not in combat, Scandinavian warriors carried their round shields on their back, thanks to a leather belt that was attached to the wooden handle.

The defensive equipment of a Viking warrior was completed by his helmet and his armour. Because these were very costly, only the richest individuals or the professional warriors could afford them. Early Scandinavian helmets belonged to the so-called *spangenhelm* type, consisting of four iron plates nailed together by several metal strips that formed a sort of frame. The term *spangen* meant 'braces' or 'strips'. This kind of helmet had a conical conformation that curved with the natural shape of the head and culminated in a point on the top, which could be spiked and was frequently adorned with coloured feathers. The front of the Viking *spangenhelm* usually included a half-facial mask consisting of a loose nose-protector attached to two metal strips designed to cover the profile of the eyebrows. The shape of the eye protection resembled that of modern eyeglass frames, and thus the helmets with a half-facial mask are also known as 'spectacle helmets'. Full facial masks were quite rare to find. Sometimes, metal check-plates and a neck protector made of chainmail could also be applied to this model of helmet. The facial mask and the frame could be made of bronze or brass, and could be heavily decorated with incisions. A magnificent surviving example of the Viking *spangenhelm* is the so-called Gjermundbu Helmet, which has a quite round shape instead of a conical one. In later Viking times, the kind of helmet described above started to be replaced by a new one which was obtained from a single piece of iron. The new helmets, commonly known as 'nasal helmets', had the same conical shape and point as the previous ones, but did not have spikes. Instead of the half-facial mask, they had a simple nasal protecting the nose, which was sometimes attached to a ridge running around the bottom edge of the helmet. The 'nasal helmets' became popular during the late Viking Age and were later used by the Normans. The famous helmets with horns, reproduced in many depictions of the Vikings from the Romantic period, are a modern invention. Although some examples of bronze horned helmets are known, these date back to the Nordic Bronze Age and were used only during ceremonies.

The great majority of the Western Vikings who had armour wore a chainmail, i.e. a protection for the torso obtained from a web of small iron rings. This 'coat of mail' was very expensive, corresponding to the cost of a shield, spear, sword and helmet put together. Consequently, only the richest warlords and the professional warriors wore chainmail. Half of the rings of a chainmail were closed, while the others were open as their ends had to be nailed together in order to close the circle. Due to these technical features, producing a coat of mail was a work of precision that required the use of several specialized tools. Many thousands of rings had to be inter-connected in order to create a single chainmail coat. They could be produced in a short version (*stuttr*) or in a long version (*sidr*). The former stopped at the level of the hips and was short-sleeved, while the latter reached to the mid-thigh or even as far as the knees and was long-sleeved. The Eastern Vikings, especially those of the Kievan Rus', preferred using lamellar armour. This consisted of hundreds of oblong iron plates that were laced together with straps or sewn to a stout fabric or leather shirt. The majority of the lamellar cuirasses covered only the torso, but some of them could be extended down over the hips and thighs. Sometimes, the shoulders and the upper-arms could also be covered. The *lamellae* could be reinforced by a mid-rib and could also be decorated with gold or silver. The members of the famous Varangian Guard were mostly equipped with lamellar armour, as were the rest of the Byzantine Army. The majority of the Vikings were not rich enough to have a chainmail or a lamellar cuirass, so instead they wore textile armour made from organic materials that was very cheap and easy to produce. This consisted of several layers of padded cloth and could be as thick as 1cm. It was usually also worn by the richest warriors, under their chainmail or lamellar cuirass. Linen, hemp canvas and woollen felt were usually used to produce textile armour, which was reinforced by parallel rows of stitches running through all the layers.

Generally speaking, the Vikings preferred fighting in tight formations stretched out in lines, in order to overlap their shields and form a defensive wall in case of enemy attack. A line could be dense or sparsely manned, depending on how long it had to be and how many warriors were available. The depth of a defensive formation was usually between five and eight lines. The most experienced and better-equipped

Viking warriors were deployed in the front line, with the main task of those in the rear lines being just to plug gaps in the front line. Shoulder-to-shoulder 'shield walls' were an effective defensive formation, especially when supported by a large number of archers. The archers could in this case fire their arrows from behind the round shields of the spear-wielding warriors. Like the Germanic peoples, the Vikings defended in line and attacked in column. An attacking column usually consisted of thirty men, being six men long and five men deep. Its numerical composition thus corresponded to that of a warship's crew. When attacked, a single column could be rapidly transformed into a 'shield column' if the warriors in its outer ranks overlapped their shields as a wall around the whole column. When the impact with the charging enemy was imminent, the warriors in the front rank squatted down and held their shields upright on the ground, while those in the second rank hold their shields above the squatting warriors. The inside ranks covered the top of this effective 'tortoise' formation. When attacking, a column was deployed in a very aggressive tactical formation known as a *svinefylkring* or 'boar's snout'. This was a wedge formation that worked in a very simple but effective way. It had the shape of an equilateral triangle, with the commander being at the apex. The best warriors were deployed near the apex, while those with little combat experience were placed at the back of the formation. The chosen warriors of the first ranks followed the movements of their commander

Front of a Viking round shield. (*Photo and copyright by Jomsborg Vikings Hird*)

Front of a
Viking round
shield. (*Photo
and copyright
by Sjórvaldar
Vikings*)

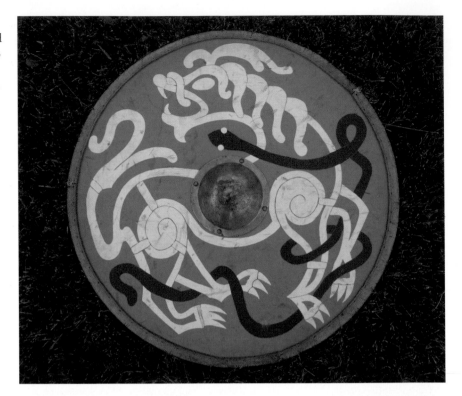

Back of a
Viking round
shield. (*Photo
and copyright
by Sjórvaldar
Vikings*)

very closely, and were in turn followed by the warriors of the other ranks. As a result, the formation could move very rapidly and was extremely flexible. If stopped by the resistance of the enemy, the attacking wedge rapidly turned into a more solid rectangle, with the warriors of the rear ranks advancing to support those who were near the apex. The *svinefylkring* was perfect to attack an enemy wall of shields at a precise point, but was exposed to counter-attacks on the flanks. After breaking the enemy line, the wedge formation attacked the opponents on the right and on the left from the rear. All movements were coordinated thanks to the presence of musicians and standard-bearers on the battlefield. The musicians played long horns to transmit orders, while the standard-bearers indicated the position of the formation's leader. Scandinavian military forces carried small triangular banners as well as impressive standards of the *draco* type (which produced a terrifying noise when the wind passed through them). In the Viking world, horses were not used for military purposes, and thus no cavalry troops existed. Horses were, however, a status symbol and a means of transport for those few nobles who were rich enough to own one of them.

Viking kaftan. (*Photo and copyright by Jomsborg Vikings Hird*)

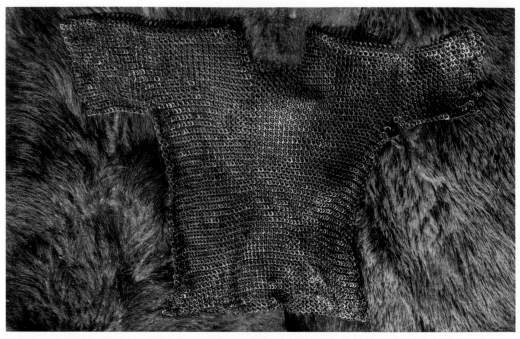

Viking chainmail. (*Photo and copyright by Jomsborg Vikings Hird*)

Viking lamellar corselet. (*Photo and copyright by Jomsborg Vikings Hird*)

Bibliography

Barraclough, E.R., *Beyond the Northlands: Viking Voyages and the Old Norse Sagas* (Oxford University Press, 2016).

Brink, S. & Price, N.S., *The Viking World* (Routledge, 2008).

Cannan, F., *Galloglass 1250–1600* (Osprey Publishing, 2010).

Cassard, J.C., *Le Siècle Des Vikings En Bretagne* (Editions Jean-Paul Gisserot, 1996).

Cavill, P., *Vikings: Fear and Faith* (Zondervan, 2001).

D'Amato, R., *The Varangian Guard 988–1453* (Osprey Publishing, 2010).

Duczko, W., *Viking Rus: Studies on the Presence of Scandinavians in Eastern Europe* (Brill, 2004).

Franklin, S. & Shepard, J., *The Emergence of Rus, 750–1200* (Longman, 1996).

Graham-Campbell, J., Hall, R.A. & Jesch, J., *Vikings and the Danelaw* (Oxbow, 2001).

Harrison, M., *Viking Hersir 793–1066* (Osprey Publishing, 1993).

Heath, I., *Armies of Feudal Europe 1066–1300* (Wargames Research Group, 1989).

Heath, I., *Armies of the Dark Ages 600–1066* (Wargames Research Group, 1980).

Heath, I., *Byzantine Armies 886–1118* (Osprey Publishing, 1979).

Heath, I., *The Vikings* (Osprey Publishing, 1985).

Hjardar, K. & Vegard, V., *Vikings at War* (Casemate, 2019).

Holman, K., *The Northern Conquest: Vikings in Britain and Ireland* (Signal, 2007).

Jesch, J., *The Scandinavians from the Vendel Period to the Tenth Century: An Ethnographic Perspective* (Boydell, 2002).

Jones, G., *A History of the Vikings* (Oxford University Press, 1968).

Lavelle, R., *Alfred's Wars: Sources and Interpretations of Anglo-Saxon Warfare in the Viking Age* (Boydell, 2010).

Lindholm, D. & Nicolle, D., *Medieval Scandinavian Armies 1100–1300* (Osprey Publishing, 2003).

Logan, F.D., *The Vikings in History* (Routledge, 1995).

Nicolle, D., *Armies of Medieval Russia 750–1250* (Osprey Publishing, 1999).

Nicolle D., *Arthur and the Anglo-Saxon Wars* (Osprey Publishing, 1984).

Oliver, N., *The Vikings* (Pegasus, 2013).

Williams, G., *Weapons of the Viking Warrior* (Osprey Publishing, 2019).

Winroth, A., *The Age of the Vikings* (Princeton University Press, 2014).

Wise, T., *Saxon, Viking and Norman* (Osprey Publishing, 1979).

The Re-enactors who Contributed to this Book

Jomsborg Vikings Hird

Greetings from the Jomsborg Vikings Hird – brotherhood of warriors from Warsaw, Poland. We attempt to recreate the tradition of the Jomsvikings, who formerly were in the pay of the Polish King Boleslaw, known in the sagas as Burisleif. Our Hird has existed since 1998, and its headquarters is in Jomsborg. The Fortress of Jomsborg is now situated in Warsaw between the Polish Olympic Centre and the Grota-Roweckiego Bridge. Our Hirdmen come mainly from Warsaw, but we also have Hirdmen from Denmark or Ukraine. The main target of our activity is the international brotherhood, but we also want to present connections between Poland and the Viking World, which were intensive. We began building our first fortress in April 2003 and, after seven months of hard toil, the basic works had been completed. Since that time, we have tried to make Jomsburg more attractive by adding new constructions and decorations (sculptures). The new fort was moved from Rynia to Warsaw in the summer of 2010. It is twice as big as the old fort, and now occupies an area of 2,000 square metres. There are eight replicas of historical buildings in the fort. We had moved only two buildings from the old fort to the new site: the Longhouse and the Valhalla Tavern. The rest has been built from new materials. The Fortress of Jomsborg is officially protected and supported by The State Archeological Museum in Warsaw. Our ship – named *Jomsborg* – is 65 per cent of the original size of the ship from Gokstad, being 15.4m long and 3.25m wide. The height from keel to bulwark rail at midships is 1.5m and the mast height is 11m. *Jomsborg* is equipped with 64 square metres of sail (which can accelerate the ship up to 10 knots with good weather conditions) and twelve pairs of oars. The crew comprises twenty-four oarsmen plus steersmen. The ship weighs about 9 tons and its draught is 0.8m. It is built of oak, with sail and rigging made out of flax.

Contacts:
E-mail: einar@jomsborg.pl
Website: www.jomsborg.pl
Facebook: https://www.facebook.com/jomsborgvikingshird/

Brokkar Lag

Brokkar Lag is based in the city of Barcelona (in Catalonia, Spain). The origin of the group dates back to 2008, when some friends formed a group for historical re-enactment based on the Viking era. Its identity goes beyond weekly training or the rigour of recreation, since members have developed effective bonds that lead them to take care of each other and to have fun together in their daily lives. Brokkar Lag attends events throughout Europe, the most important of which are at Moesgard (Denmark) and Wolin (Poland). Every September, Brokkar Lag holds its annual training weekend (BLOD OG VIN), attended by re-enactors from all over Europe. Brokkar belongs to the Jomsborg brotherhood, attached to their South Storm. We feel like authentic twenty-first-century Vikings who have turned their hobby into a lifestyle.

Contacts:
Facebook: https://www.facebook.com/brokkarlag/?__xts__

Sjórvaldar Vikings

Sjórvaldar Vikings are a non-profit organization whose primary focus is dedicated to enriching the educational experience through immersive living history. Sjórvaldar was founded by those with a shared interest and passion for the history, crafts and battle elements of all things Scandinavian, with the intention and commitment to share it with the public with as much authenticity as possible. Members aim to depict a mobile, seasonal camp/temporary village complete with living quarters, work spaces and recreational areas. The village not only showcases the lifestyle and culture of the period, but also the harsher and battle-ready aspects of life in what was known as the Viking Age, specifically the tenth century. With a thoughtful training regimen and regular training sessions, members learn the ins and outs of planning and performing a safe, entertaining and as close to real as possible combat display, without jeopardizing our personal safety. At our events, we strive to a high standard of presentation, historical accuracy and attention to detail with all endeavours, whether with active demonstrations or displays. Our presentations are based upon archaeological and literary research. From weaving to blacksmithing, woodworking and everything in between, members enjoy sharing their skills with and educating the public by demonstrating live period crafts as they would have been practised during the Viking Age.

Contacts:
E-mail: sjorvaldarvikings@gmail.com
Website: https://www.sjorvaldar.com/
Facebook: https://www.facebook.com/sjorvaldar/

Confraternita del Leone/Historia Viva

La 'Confraternita del Leone' è un'associazione culturale di ricostruzione storica, con l'obiettivo di studiare, rivivere e divulgare la storia lombarda, con particolare attenzione a quella di Brescia e delle popolazioni che l'hanno abitata nei secoli. Le ricerche dei nostri studiosi spaziano senza limiti nella ricca e complessa storia locale, concentrando l'aspetto rievocativo e didattico sui periodi dal IV al I secolo a.C. in cui furono protagonisti Reti, Celti e Romani, quindi sul secolo VIII dei Longobardi, sull'età dei Comuni e delle Signorie del XII e XIII secolo e infine sul XVII secolo e l'epoca dei Buli sotto la Repubblica di Venezia. La ricerca storica della *Confraternita del Leone* si articola su tre differenti e complementari piattaforme di studio, la cui finalità è raggiungere dei risultati di globalità analitica in grado di estrinsecare degli spaccati storici di corretta filologicità e, ove possibile, di assoluto realismo e scientificità: istituto di ricerca storica, laboratori di archeologia sperimentale e accademia di antiche arti marziali occidentali. Nel partecipare ad eventi storici la *Confraternita del Leone* allestisce un accampamento di circa 500 metri quadrati, dispone di vari antichi mestieri dimostrativi con artigiani all'opera tra cui il fabbro con la forgia, la tessitura a telaio, la macinazione di cereali, l'usbergaro, lo speziale, il cerusico, la zecca, il cambiavalute, il cacciatore, l'arcaio, lo scrivano, l'avvocato e il fabbricante di candele; in battaglia sono schierati arcieri, balestrieri, fanteria, ariete, trabucchi e mantelletti.

Contacts:
E-mail: confraternitadelleone@gmail.com
Website: http://www.confraternitaleone.com/

Index